CREATIVE STRATEGIES

10 APPROACHES TO SOLVING *more than* DESIGN PROBLEMS

Fridolin Beisert

FOR MY THREE GIRLS:
Wakako, Satchi, and Coco

SPECIAL THANKS

TO THOSE WHO HAVE HELPED ME ALONG THIS JOURNEY:

My family: Heide, Michael, and Florian

Impactful teachers: Scott and Neville

Creative catalysts: Jared and Walid

Tree-house gang: Norm and Marty

Partner in crime: Karen

Inspiring influencers: Kan and Goose

Red Thread team: Fredi, Matthias, and Vlad

Illustrator: Jessie

Cover design: Tomo

Foreword: Andrew

Awesome Design Studio Press team: Tinti, Teena, and Prances

And to my countless students who continuously inspire me to be a better teacher

CONTENTS

= Timeline   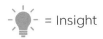 = Insight   = Tip

FOREWORD

As a product designer, I often question what types of products we really need in this world. In the end, products are marketed for people, and as creators of these products, we, as designers, try to satiate their tastes accordingly. There are many types of people: some may have reserved tastes, others have flashy taste, or some have no specific taste at all. Since becoming equipped with Fridolin Beisert's creative strategies, I'm no longer concerned with satisfying tastes. Rather, I ask myself if it's possible to eliminate this "productization" of taste and focus on redefining the idea of taste.

I first met Frido when I took his class, Creative Strategies. It was one of the last classes I took while I attended ArtCenter College of Design, and I was skeptical that my creative approach would be drastically changed as a senior. But if it weren't for his class, I would have never approached design the way I do today. I was once obsessed with the idea of creating things that were simply "different," because that's what I thought creativity was. My work felt ephemeral and unnecessary in this world. I felt frustrated and wondered what I was doing wrong. Things changed when I took his class. I discovered a newfound clarity and began to see paths to a solution that I was previously blind to. It turned out that the mechanics behind creativity could be distilled into classes and be taught. And now, with his *Creative Strategies* book, anyone can benefit from Frido's valuable approaches and lessons, whether you're in the creative field or not.

Understanding the creative process brought me confidence, leading to fearlessness, a word I normally wouldn't use to describe myself. Once, I even showed up to Frido's class with a completed assignment that had nothing to do with what he asked for: I rebranded Microsoft when he asked the class to redefine what a popsicle could be. It gained so much attention that I even ended up getting hired at Microsoft. Decisions like this were risky, maybe even foolish, but they helped me realize that fear of failure was one of the biggest barriers for me to grow as a designer. Once fear was removed from my process, I was left with the freedom to explore and reevaluate the framing of design problems.

Today, as a working professional, I can look back and recognize how his class has helped me mature as both a designer and a person. Frido's teachings have become the foundation of my creative process, and I hope this book will inspire you in a similar way.

Andrew Kim

Designer at Apple

LAUNCH

A design student once asked me a very challenging question: **"Can you teach me how to be more creative?"**

In my line of work as an educator I get challenging questions all the time, but this one was different. It stuck with me. Probably because I did not give a very good answer. In fact, I can't remember if I had an answer at all at the time. I may have mumbled something incoherent like, "You just need to try harder . . ." And that was not good enough. The question has haunted me ever since. I knew I had to go on a quest to provide an answer.

Until that point I had never given much thought to how anyone learns to be creative. I saw the act of being creative as a choice rather than a skill. We all have brains comprised of two cerebral hemispheres that are supposed to allow us to think both logically and creatively. To me, being creative was simply choosing to have both halves work together as a team. No special assembly required and batteries already included. If I wanted to apply creativity to my work, then I would make that a conscious decision. But by digging deeper I realized that perhaps it *is* a skill that I have learned, maybe I just didn't realize how. So how did I learn the skill of being creative? To find an answer I started by analyzing the evolution of my own design process.

My time as a student at ArtCenter College of Design has taught me that any skill can be learned. It just takes two key ingredients: time and good instructions—and perhaps a healthy dose of effort as the catalyst. Germans have a proverb, "Übung macht den Meister," which translates to, "Practice makes perfect." This pretty much summarizes my time at ArtCenter: try, fail, repeat.

As long as I didn't stop this process, any skill was attainable, regardless of my initial talent level. My teachers pushed me to the very edge of what I thought I was capable of. Some of them pushed me even further, and for that I am forever grateful. Once I understood that just about anything could be learned this way, I felt that I had stumbled into a never-ending source of energy to fuel the learning process. As a result of this relentless training, I have seen myself accomplish designs in my professional career that otherwise would not have been possible.

I once gave a talk to incoming design students about what my educational experience was like and what they might expect. I shared just how incredibly hard and difficult learning to design can be, how students work longer hours than in any other discipline that I know of, and that they better not expect to have a social life outside of the school environment. My talk started to sound like a serious warning to avoid design school, so I scrambled to conclude my presentation on a positive note. I said that what you put in (the "hard work and passion") is what you get out (the "learning"). I got blank stares from the audience. So I tried a different way:

"The most important thing that I have learned is that I could achieve anything I want in life, as long as I set my mind to it."

That did it. I think that this perfectly summarizes what any great education is supposed to do, which is to empower you to go out into the world and make the most of your time in a meaningful way. In my case, learning how to be a designer came with a positive side effect: it taught me how to become an excellent problem solver. That does not mean that I always have good ideas. (My peers would probably confirm that most of my ideas are rather silly.) Rather, it means that I *know* that any problem can be solved creatively using the skills and processes that I have learned.

After graduating from ArtCenter, I cofounded a boutique design consultancy called Red Thread with three friends whom I met in school. We all had different majors and brought varied skill sets together that allowed us to work across disciplines. We worked on design projects ranging in scale from graphic to product design, from fashion photography to music videos, and from interior designs to live events. We took on any project that interested us. We were not too concerned *if* we could design something, only *how*. Somewhat appropriately our tagline was, "Think tank with a toolbox," indicating that we could come up with ideas and also have the necessary skills to turn them into reality.

As I was looking through our body of work, I noticed that there was a relatively small percentage of truly *creative* projects. That felt a bit humbling. Most of the designs were well executed, just not worth mentioning in the context of creativity (unless you are really into style guides for car companies). What stood out though was something else, the quantity: more than 350 projects in the course of about seven years.

That was the clue I needed: I had learned creativity through a process of quantity. I had never felt that I was an expert on the psychological side of creativity. Thankfully I have a bit more mileage on the practical side. I realized that the creative process *is* a skill and that it can be practiced, just like riding a bicycle. And in my case I just needed to find the right bicycle to test this theory. Since I believe in learning by doing, I enrolled in graduate school to prototype methods on how to teach creativity. Two years later, I was ready to launch the strategies.

Each of the creative strategies featured in this book has a distinct name that I use to describe the process. You are probably familiar with some of the terminology, or have come across similar principles in other environments or contexts. I consistently use all of these methods in my own creative work, so hopefully some of them will be beneficial to your line of work as well.

Some of the designs described were done for clients, some were done for myself, some were done to prove a point, and even others were done just because I felt like it. I omitted most references to organizations or individuals to make the essence of the story the hero.

Collectively, the 10 creative strategies are about using both the right and left hemispheres of the brain simultaneously and in harmony, responding to the challenge with a flexible mind. That flexibility, looking at each design problem as a chance to learn something new, will yield consistent advances in creative output. I see evidence of that regularly in my classroom, where students with an open-minded approach produce far greater creative leaps in their work. Of course, many of their projects still end up in conceptual failure—just like real life.

Creativity is a skill that can be learned by exercising both sides of the brain regularly. To you, who are reading this: I hope that these strategies will help you on your own journey just as they have helped me on mine. And to my student that asked me the question: I am sorry it took me so long to put this together.

Cheers,

Fridolin T. Beisert
Yakushima, Japan

CREATIVE STRATEGIES

Creativity is a verb.

Before we dive into the 10 strategies, let's start with the elephant in the room: what is creativity? We intuitively *know* when something is creative the moment we see it. It is accompanied with a burst of feeling amazed, inspired, and perhaps even emotional. These are, of course, just reactions. I combed through the writings of people who are much smarter than I am and distilled a definition that describes creativity as a process:

Creativity is solving problems with new solutions that have value.

Embedded in this attempt are three main components that are important for the context of this book. The first is solving problems. In the field of design, everything is a problem, and not necessarily in the sense of being "problematic" or "causing harm." Sometimes something as simple (or difficult) as choosing a color can be a problem. It is just the way we like to talk about what we do. There are multiple ways to start a given design problem, but they always have one thing in common: they have a question at the origin (the "problem") and an answer as the result (the "solution").

The next component in the definition is the word *new*. This is where things get interesting. The first time you do *anything* that relates to creativity, it will always be seen as being creative because it is *new*. Our daughter recently drew a picture of our family, and we were so thrilled that we put it up on the wall. We think she is going to be the next Picasso, never mind that we look like stick figures. But she is only four years old, and this was her first creative expression! Now fast-forward 15 years: what if she creates a similar drawing in content and style? It would no longer be new. It could almost be a reason to be concerned. It would probably not get her into art school, despite my ties.

The term *new* is relative to time (hat tip to Einstein).

Doing a similar type of work over a long period of time is not considered being creative. In order to stay creative, you need to produce new work. This is actually embedded in the word itself: creativity comes from the Latin term *creo* and simply refers to *create* or *make*. So if you want to be more creative you have to make more work and try new approaches. Don't just throw pasta against the wall and call it being creative just because you *created* a mess—even if it is the first time that you have done it.

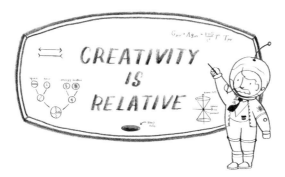

The final component of the definition is the word *value*. This one is relative to space (another hat tip to Einstein). You can create a new painting in your studio, and if the result makes you happy, then this is of positive value. You can show it to your friends and they may not like it, and that is negative value. Likewise, you can create a new mechanism for a product, and if it functions, it is of positive value; if it fails, it is of negative value. In essence, anything you create needs some form of an evaluation at the end. At ArtCenter we call this a critique, or crit for short. These can be subjective crits ("I like it!") or objective crits ("It works!"). And every project has this step as part of the creative process.

People who have achieved a certain level of respect through their bodies of work or accomplishments will be happy to tell you how many steps it took them to get there. Those who are labeled "creative" have worked very hard to reach that level. They create not because they want to be successful but because they want to change the world around them. The many diverse creatives whom I have had the pleasure to meet all have one common characteristic: passion for what they do.

And it is this passion that drives them to be curious and to turn that curiosity into sheer relentless activity and productivity. Some have called this concept simply grit. Creatives do things because they want to and not because they have to. While I believe that creativity is a skill that can be learned, the element of passion is something that each person needs to find within herself or himself. Of course the irony here is that you need to be curious in order to detect and continuously find your passion for creative output. If you are not curious, then you are not in a seeking mode, and thus finding something that ignites your passion becomes at best a game of chance. Having a healthy dose of passion and curiosity has become the only prerequisite that I ask students to bring in preparation for learning Creative Strategies. And, of course, a pencil and some paper.

DIGGING DEEPER

Question everything.

As I started to analyze the big "aha" moments in my creative journeys, I uncovered that at the core of each critical juncture in my development as a designer there has been a series of questions that did not appear magically, but instead were part of a system of cause and effect. And those pivotal questions always followed the same pattern: they were born of *curiosity*, followed by *inquiry*, and eventually taken into *action*.

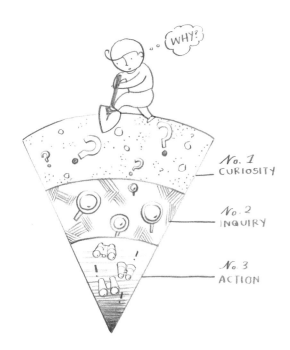

WHY?

No. 1
CURIOSITY

No. 2
INQUIRY

No. 3
ACTION

See, I believe that you should always pose three questions when faced with a problem or a project: it is the most powerful strategy to start toward becoming more creative. The exact *type* of question will, of course, vary depending on the situation. Here's a potential list of three questions for you to ask yourself when confronting a new challenge:

QUESTION 1

is about curiosity, what piques your interest:
Why is it the way it is?

QUESTION 2

is one of inquiry, when one tries to understand the variables:
How does it work?

QUESTION 3

implies some form of action:
What can I make of it?

I ask these questions constantly. And I have learned to treasure those moments when I decide to go and answer the third one. To me it always implies the first step of a creative journey, and it is how I steered toward the field of design.

IDENTIFYING THE BLIND SPOT

In the novel *The Hitchhiker's Guide to the Galaxy* by Douglas Adams, there is a group of beings that are trying to find out the answer to what they believe is a fundamental question:

What is the meaning of life?

For this purpose, they build an immense super computer called Deep Thought, feed it the question, and wait. They wait for 7.5 million years for Deep Thought to compute and then check and verify the answer. Finally, the big moment arrives and Deep Thought reveals the answer to the eager crowd: "42."

Everyone panics because they have waited so long for the answer, and though they have it, nobody understands what it means. Deep Thought goes on to explain that another more powerful super computer would be able to answer what the meaning of the number 42 is, and that it would take 10 million years to process. Eventually that attempt also backfires as the second computer is destroyed five minutes before finishing the calculation to make way for a super galactic highway.

I love this part of the story because of the sheer magnitude of effort and time invested in seeking *one* useful answer. Fans of the book have since created complex theories that try to illustrate what the number could represent. (When asked, the author later admitted that when he wrote the story he chose the number 42 at random). What I realized about my own work after reading the story is that I *always* start my project with a question—a question that is the child of preceding questions. Just like the beings in the novel, I am searching for some form of a meaningful answer; the only difference is that I ask many more questions to get to the right one.

 We don't have the time to sit and wait for random answers.

When starting a design project, I am generally not concerned with what I can see or where things are going; I am much more interested in what I *can't* see and what I might be missing. It has led me to actively *seek* the blind spot, the area that I know I am overlooking. I know that whatever is in plain sight of my research might be a way to start, but it is probably not the solution to the design problem. I know that I need to dig deeper and go beneath the surface. That is where I find unexpected solutions that bring new life to my designs.

Every project that I have been involved in has these blind spots; actually most situations in life have these subtle areas that are just out of plain sight but could make a big difference if they were taken into consideration. You are probably aware of the term *blind spot* from driving a vehicle, referring to an area that is undetectable by regular mirrors, yet it exists right beside you. It is the physical closeness that makes it a blind spot. However, I am referring to the anatomical use of the term, which is a little different. In human anatomy, it describes a small region of the retina where vision is not experienced. This is because in that area the actual fibers from the optic nerve emerge from the eyeball, and thus no visual images can be transmitted.

Our brain has managed to compensate for this blocked-out area by patching it over. Thankfully, we are unaware of its existence. I try to look at design problems the same way. They all have blind spots that we cannot detect with the naked eye, and perhaps we are better off not seeing them. That is my starting point to dig deeper and try to uncover areas that others can't see. I don't stop asking questions after the first one. In my design process I am actively in seeking mode.

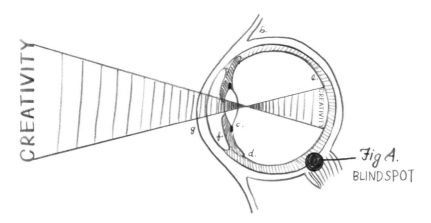

Fig A.
BLINDSPOT

Maybe it is just a form of curiosity, but I love asking questions. I try to ask questions that no one else is asking. I try to look where no one else is looking. These questions are sometimes silly or even immature, but I like to bring them to the light. My young daughter also does this very well. She can ask, "Why?" until infinity happens.

Like any child, she is just naturally curious about the world around her. As she grows up, I hope she will add two more levels to her line of questioning: inquiry and, ultimately, action. In combination with curiosity, they are the tools needed to dig deeper and start the journey of learning how to be more creative.

THREE QUESTIONS IN ACTION

Turning a Loss at the "Allwin" Machine into a Win

When I was a young teenager, my parents took me on a trip to visit friends in Great Britain, and as part of the vacation we went to a historical outdoor museum that was like a time warp back to the heart of the Industrial Revolution. I vividly remember going into an old pharmacy and seeing all of the beautiful packaging designs and bottles on shelves behind the handcrafted display counter. There was also an old coal mine shaft there, together with the steam-powered machinery and original tools that were used by the miners. The highlight, though, was going to the amusement area that featured traditional candy, funny mirrors, and a working penny arcade.

In one of the corners of the arcade was a machine that looked a bit like a vertical pinball machine. When I inserted a coin in it, it released a steel ball that I would then launch into a field of nails with the hopes of landing it in one of multiple holes that could win me a free game and coin. I was amazed, not so much by the machine but more by the fact that it didn't use electricity at all: it was all based on mechanics and gravity.

After losing all my pocket money, I asked Question 1:

What is this thing?

The attendant told me that these types of machines are referred to as Allwins. The name did not exactly correspond with my experience of losing money; I was really curious to learn how this thing worked, so I asked the attendant Question 2:

Could you open it for me so I can see the inside?

The inside was surprisingly simple, because the main objective was to either win or lose, and most attempts resulted in the latter. I took a blurry picture for reference. I asked my parents if I could have one of these machines, and they were wise enough to decline my request. That caused me to dig deeper.

My next question was more for myself, because after looking at the pictures that I took, I realized that the actual play value of the game became a bit boring after awhile. It also was no fun to lose all my money. There was no story, no action–reaction and no risk–reward elements, which led me to Question 3: ·

I wonder if I can design a better one?

It took me nearly two years for me to finish my own version of the Allwin machine, using only a power drill, a jigsaw, some wood, nails, and glass for the cover. I would work on it after school, on weekends, and regularly show the progress

to one of my best friends, who would play it and point out what could use improvement. These were the critiques needed to advance the play value. After I was finally done, I had, in a way, answered that third question for myself, but I did not know at the time that this machine represented an important stepping-stone in my career.

I was finishing up school in Germany, and it was time to figure out what to do with my life. I had a memorable session together with my father whereby he would ask me questions to find out what my passions were and how to best connect them to a path. I think at the time he concluded that I should go to a developing nation and build water wells because I like to help people, experience new cultures, and I enjoy making things. It turns out that he, in essence, was not too far off, even though some of the details of my path turned out to be very different. I ended up deciding to apply to a design school in America to learn how to make things that could help people. During my interview for the school, I showed my portfolio and was asked if I had any project that demonstrated technical knowledge. That is when I handed out coins to everyone and had them play with my machine. I got accepted.

Increasing the Worth of a Dollar Bill

Even though leaving Germany to learn how to become a designer was an important developmental step in my creative career, I frequently reach to my cultural roots for inspiration. There is a beautiful word in the German language, *Untersuchung*, which means a form of investigation, but literally translated it would be "to search underneath." Searching for something—even if you are not sure what it is—can lead to interesting insights that otherwise would have never surfaced. The accumulation of these insights builds a knowledge base of experiences that fosters the process of creativity. They do not always need to be projects that serve a particular purpose; they can sometimes be experiments that are open-ended when it comes to interpreting the results. This was the case when I wanted to find out the price of an ordinary dollar bill.

I have always been fascinated with coins, probably because of my passion for machines, especially coin-operated ones. I do not have any interest in collecting coins; I only like what they represent as an action, not as a passive object. So when

I came across a very unique old penny, I had another one of those three-question moments. At the time I had been cleaning my studio, and sold a few devices over the Internet, and was always surprised just how much some things would sell for. So when I looked at the vintage penny, I asked myself Question 1:

I wonder how much this penny is worth?

Don't hold your breath; I found out quickly that it was worth exactly one penny. But I did find other coins, real collectibles that were selling for a whole lot more than their face value. Which turned into Question 2, that of inquiry:

Why do people pay more than face value for an object?

In general terms, the answer is relatively easy: people pay for what they think it is worth to *them*, what they perceive as the *value*. Value, of course is as relative for each individual as is creativity. Value can be either the function (what a design does) or the form (how meaningful the design is). In the case of the coins that were being sold, it was all about the rarity and the story (form); the face value (function) was somewhat irrelevant. Which made me wonder if it is possible to add value to an object by giving it a story. Thus, Question 3 was:

Is it possible to sell an ordinary dollar bill for more than it is worth?

It is of course illegal to "sell" money for more than its value, so I thought about declaring the auction as art. I loosely quoted Frank Lloyd Wright by writing, "If it sells, it's art," on the dollar bill. (I was told afterward that writing on money is also illegal).

This became the core of the auction's description that outlined my thought process. I explained that I have an ordinary dollar bill and that I was conducting an experiment to see how much it would be worth, considering it is not special in any way. It was a very thorough and long description that probably helped the auction because the dollar sold for a winning bid of $17.50.

My friends immediately suggested trying the experiment again with a $100 bill, but I had already found the answer to my question. More importantly, though,

I learned that the people were not bidding on the actual item or the function that it represented. They were curious to help me find the answer to my question. They bid on it because they wanted to be part of the experiment, and they connected to the story of the auction. Stories always sell.

Sometimes you need to go out and find the kind of design problems that you want to solve for by yourself. This is a form of "problem finding" that turns ordinary creatives into design investigators. Exercised regularly, this fuels curiosity and creates a thirst for the discovery of new insights. Admittedly, it is not easy to be constantly seeking because there is the reality of pressing deadlines, full inboxes, and not having enough physical resources. But how much fun is that kind of life? I made it a priority to sometimes question my priorities.

 One of the beautiful side effects of this investigative approach to life is that it can help you become a lifelong learner.

You will learn more about yourself and more about your surroundings. It will help you build experience and stepping-stones that elevate your career, even if it may not seem so at the time. I find that if I am not creating, I am not just standing still, I am actually stagnating—slowly reversing the process of being creative into just thinking about how to react to life as it passes by. That is also what keeps me motivated: it is not necessarily finding the next design to work on but rather to find the next question that I want to answer.

MARINATING IDEAS

I feel very fortunate that my parents have always nurtured both the analytical and creative sides of my mind. I don't think they did that on purpose; it was perhaps influenced by their respective occupations. My father is a doctor and my mother is a children's book illustrator and painter. These two professions to me represent two distinctly different thinking patterns: left brain for the analytical side of a doctor who is trying to find the cause of a pain point, and right brain for the creative side of an illustrator who is telling a story. However, I don't think it is possible to isolate the hemispheres and to claim that one side is solely responsible for either way of thinking. I see proof of this in my father. Even though he studied to be a doctor, he is an equally good artist and designer. I like to think that he represents a fine example of "left-brain creativity," and he continuously inspires me to create.

Yet, despite my urge to exercise my creative mind regularly, when I am sitting by myself in front of a white piece of paper, I have no ideas. None. A lot of great artists and designers love and praise the white piece of paper, but I cannot do much with it other than to fold it into a paper airplane. I need a seed, a starting point, a word, a concept, an idea—anything really. I have learned that I do not get a starting point by sitting in front of a piece of paper. Even when I want to only do a drawing, I first need to think of what to draw, otherwise the actual drawing lacks meaning.

Knowing that about myself, I have made a habit of collecting all my ideas, concepts, and thoughts whenever and wherever they happen. It makes them easily accessible when I sit down to produce something new. What is more, I believe that through the process of writing things down, my mind has time to process the information first. I call this magic process "marinating ideas" because, through the passage of time, thoughts have time to mature. Actually, the idea might still be the same, but I know what needs to be added and what needs to be removed to develop it further.

There is yet another great German word, *Überlegen*, which as a verb translates to "think" and as an adjective to being "superior." I believe that this is a wonderful duality to describe the process and result of marinating ideas. The human mind, especially the subconscious portion, is a very powerful processor of information. When it is idle, it is combing through lines of code and puts them in some kind of order. It can repair broken links by connecting and combining strings of data in new ways. But for me, it only works if the information is loaded properly into the brain, and writing ideas down is a great method to do this.

There is a happy side effect to this method, which is that once I document an idea, it frees up my mind so that I can focus on what I am currently working on. I don't label my ideas as being "right" or "wrong." Instead I write them down with the thought of "not right now." I can temporarily forget them and get back to them when the time is right. This has allowed me to create a system of sustained creative productivity because I have access to a fully stocked idea vault.

 Make a habit of becoming a master documentarian of your own creative career. Record ideas and thoughts to let them marinate. That way you will have a continuous stream of wonderful art and design projects to work on for yourself. It is rocket fuel for the mind.

Adding input from trusted sources can further accelerate the process of marination. Ideas are enhanced through *conversations*. Recently my daughter's preschool teacher asked me how to create children's books. I told her that the best way for her to start would be by simply making them. *Learning by doing.* She realized that she already has an audience to read her stories to (and probably receive some very honest crits), so we discussed possible topics for the first series of books. I told her that the source of inspiration could come entirely from the children that she was teaching and caring for. She said that one of the kids had just asked her: "What if a chicken had five legs?" A good question indeed. She decided to add this question together with others into her notebook to let them marinate. Who knows? Maybe one day we will see the answer in the form of an illustrated children's book.

If you use it regularly, a creativity journal can become your depository for inspirational ideas, textures, thoughts, visuals, and concepts. I love looking at them because they are so personal. It is like a portal to the essence of a designer. A well-kept journal or notebook is rarely clean and tidy. It contains a lot of documentation, both in written, sketched, and collected form. It shows experimentation and thought in the moment, unedited and raw. There is no control Z, no edit, and no spell-check. It is what it is, and that is the beauty of it.

And then you can share that journal with friends. I bring mine to the dinner table. When I have an idea that lacks "something" that I can't see (a blind spot), I discuss it with my wife. Her perspective can bring new life to my concept and allows it to mature. Ideas are everywhere; you just need to write them down and give them time to develop.

PROBLEM FRAMING

Change the problem.

ArtCenter, the school where I teach, is located in Southern California, and we have a very unique relationship with nature. The constant perfect weather makes us feel as if we are living in paradise even though there are a number of serious natural disasters possible at any moment. We can get hurricane-like winds in the canyons, wildfires that take out entire hillsides, and occasional drizzle that seems to bring the entire infrastructure to a halt. Supposedly we also get earthquakes.

Because of all the excellent research possibilities that are available here, the topic of disaster relief is a very engaging design project for students to investigate and for which to develop solutions. They can conduct expert interviews with the various firefighters, mountain-rescue groups, and governmental institutions. They can also see and test all of the equipment that is currently in use and, most importantly, they have access to the citizens who are being directly affected by these natural disasters. Despite all of these amazing options for deep investigation of the topic, it is still possible to start off in the wrong direction. I once had a student ask me in the hallway for a crit:

"Frido, I need some feedback for my design solutions for my other class; can you help me?"

"Sure! What is your design problem?"

"Well, the project is about disaster relief and I am designing an emergency earthquake kit for the home."

"Sounds interesting! So what is the problem you are trying to solve?"

"I did some research, and my concept is to make the kit more accessible after an earthquake hits . . ."

"And you have a difficult time trying to come up with ideas on how to make it accessible after an earthquake?

"Yes, exactly! Can you help me?"

"I cannot help with that problem, because you are trying to solve the wrong one. But I can help you in finding the right question!"

The student looked at me perplexed and said, "What do you mean I have the wrong problem?"

"Maybe it is easier if I show you what the real problem is . . ."

We went to my classroom that had about 20 designers waiting for their crits to begin. I told them that I first needed them to help the student with a quick, informal survey. I asked them to raise their hands if they thought that a major earthquake is likely in the next 5–10 years. All of the hands went up. Then I asked how many of them actually had an emergency earthquake kit at home. All of the hands went down. Not one of them actually had a kit at home despite the fact that they knew an earthquake is likely to happen.

I turned around to the student who came to me and explained that the issue is not how to make a kit more accessible after an earthquake, or how to design a better earthquake kit. The real problem is how to make sure people actually have an earthquake kit in the first place. Unlike the other natural disasters that have a bit of predictability via weather forecasts, earthquakes come whenever they feel like it. And in that situation, even the best-designed product is useless if you do not *have* it. The question that he was asking was not the one that would have resulted in anything creative at all.

The student was trying to approach the wrong problem, and the concepts would have merely resulted in a Band-Aid solution. A Band-Aid solution does not solve anything really; it only tries to cover up a much deeper wound. Band-Aid solutions are everywhere if you look for them. Just think of duct tape—I use that stuff all the time; it is fantastic— it gets the job done, but it does not fix the problem at its core.

NO. 2: PROBLEM FRAMING | **Fridolin Beisert**

CORE LOCATION

Every design problem has, at its core, a question that needs to be answered with a new solution. The process of problem framing is taking a step back and exchanging the original question with a better one. *Better* is, of course, a relative term that depends on the scope and criteria of the project. In the example of the earthquake kit, it does not matter how good the design is; it is rather essential that people actually have an earthquake kit in the first place. The design problem is how to help people be better prepared.

 When it comes to reframing a problem, it is about finding the right question that leads toward a more successful solution path.

I once heard the story of a research project that was done for an athletic shoe company. The marketers wanted to identify thought leaders within different social groups. Their theory was that if a thought leader adopts a certain new trend, in this case a new style of kids' sneakers, then the members of that group would soon follow and purchase the same style. For this, all the researchers had to do was to identify the coolest kid in the neighborhood and give him or her the shoes.

The story continues that the researchers went to playgrounds and started asking around who everyone thought was the coolest kid. Every child gave the name of a new child to ask. Finally, they reached a kid who answered: "I am."

They had reached the core. And soon after handing out a pair of sneakers, everyone was wearing the same style.

Now

↑

I like this story for two reasons. First, the research team had to employ a simple method of successive questioning. They were digging deeper and deeper. The question itself was always the same one: Who is the coolest kid? And each answer got them a little bit closer to the core or the essence. The second reason why I like this story is because I believe that once you find the core of anything and change it, then everything that surrounds this core will follow it automatically. You can see this principle applied in many layers of society, but it is especially true in company structures: What the CEO says is what everyone will do. It is very difficult to change that vision from the perimeter, but very easy to influence from the center. All you have to do is to find access to that center.

When it comes to developing concepts, I always try to find that center, the essence that makes the idea an idea in the first place. I ask myself:

When the design is done, what exactly does it need to accomplish?

If the answer to that question is too vague I keep asking myself *why* until I feel that I have reached the core. From there I can eliminate any aspect, element, or path that does not help me to achieve that goal.

I once was having a business lunch with three leaders from local design consultancies. They had come to my school to recruit some talent. We discussed the typical technical and thinking skills that were needed in order to become successful designers. Toward the end of the lunch, coffee and cake were served and the discussion became casual. One of the participants looked at his watch to see how much time there was until the actual recruiting would begin. Immediately, the entire conversation switched to comparing our watches. Everyone had a timepiece to show, except me. I wasn't wearing one and felt strangely left out of the conversation.

After that day I had a few flashbacks of being picked last in just about any popularity contest. I asked myself the first question:

Which watch should I get in order to be part of the conversation?

This question is, of course, a "me too" kind of question that would inevitably result in a "me too" type of solution. Subsequently, all the ideas that fell under this path did not yield any new results. My first thought was to perhaps research and buy a very expensive watch myself, but in a way that would have been too easy, and besides, I did not have a budget to spend on this. Of course, I could have also tried to acquire a fake watch that looked expensive and exclusive, but that would have been an even worse solution. After a while I realized that none of the ideas that I had were providing any solutions that I liked, because they would all result in a temporary Band-Aid solution. I noticed that I was working on the wrong problem and I needed to exchange the problem. I asked myself:

THEN

How can my watch be the conversation?

In looking back at the lunch meeting, I noticed that while everyone was an accomplished creative in the field of design, none of them had actually *designed* his or her own watch. With that new question, I immediately knew that I needed to make my own watch. I had created a completely new path for myself to solve this problem.

All of the watches from that meeting were more or less similar. They were expensive, beautiful, and told time very accurately. Yet all we talked about was the design (the form) of each watch and not the accuracy (the function). Actually, the concept of time was never brought up. This was a huge advantage in creating a prototype, because designing a functioning watch would use a lot of resources that I did not have. I decided to create a watch that looks like a watch but would purposely *not* tell time.

I sketched out possible ideas (including one that used a miniature hourglass), but I wanted to design the prototype using existing parts. I had an old watch that I was able to take apart to use as the case. I also had a small kids' puzzle that you have to shake in order to move some steel balls into holes. I added 12 holes into the face of the watch, and put two of the balls inside the case (representing hours and minutes). Whenever I show the watch, the two balls are spinning around like crazy and randomly settle in holes. This always triggers a funny reaction where the person tries to understand the mechanism in the watch (there is none) and asks where I bought it (I didn't).

Interestingly, these two questions are about curiosity and inquiry as discussed in the previous chapter. I once had a chance to show it to one of my design idols, who is an internationally recognized design rock star. He started coming up with ideas on how to improve the design by making it functional and offered to put it in production (I politely declined his generous offer). All he was thinking about was *action*, which is the last of the three questions that are always at the core of my own creative journeys.

Locating this core has become an obsession of mine. I know that if I find the right question to answer, then the path will lead to its own finish line. In the field of design, it is easy to fall into the trap of wasting energy trying to solve *effects* of a problem by creating Band-Aid solutions. At Red Thread, when we received design briefs from clients, we would often automatically assume that they were trying to have us solve the wrong problem. In phase one of a given project, we would often change their brief so that it would have a new question at the origin. That question led us in the direction of the core location, away from the perimeter.

PARADIGM SHIFT

As any designer, I was not immune to the fact that some projects just did not seem like they would be a lot of fun to work on. But I had to do them anyway because I had already committed to them and it was too late to back out. These types of projects always reminded me of required classes that I had to take in school where, for one reason or another, I was not fully mentally present. It probably had to do with the topic, and I had to find some form of creative energy to complete the projects. I remember that in these situations I would often seek ways to create my own personal paradigm shift.

A paradigm shift represents a fundamental change in the approach to a problem. It has famously been dubbed "thinking differently." It is also aimed at questioning underlying assumptions. To that effect, the phrase "thinking differently" could also be replaced with "asking different questions," followed by a journey to answer these new questions. In school I would take a repetitive assignment, such as copying letterforms, and turn it into a quest:

What if I design my own handwriting?

When I was first learning 3D software, I challenged myself to use my left hand (I am right-handed) to control the interface:

How about I use my opposite hand to operate the computer?

In shop class, learning about fabrication tools, we had to produce a nonworking appearance model of a Ghostbuster, and I wondered:

Why not make a working model?

I created a fully functioning toy design, complete with blinking lights and green slime.

Any project can be turned into a fun activity, as long as it has an interesting question at its origin. Often it is up to you to create that question before going after it.

In my professional work, I would turn design tasks into challenges. These challenges would fuel my creative energy. I would try to design using fewer tools and resources and in less time. If the deliverable asked for a digital output, I would attempt to create it with analog tools (and vice versa). If the budget for production was very low, I would try to produce a design that would cost even less to make. That last one was not always successful.

What I have learned with this way of thinking is that you can create a league of your own, a creative playground that provides limitless opportunities for personal growth, experimentation, and knowledge that enhance your palette of skills.

When working on what might seem like an unexciting problem, go ahead and set your own goals for it.

Use it as an excuse to try a new technique, a new theme, a new collaboration, or test a new style. Go ahead and learn a new skill. Think about how you can get intrinsic motivation from working on that project (as supposed to extrinsic motivation, such as money or a grade for a class). Think to yourself:

What is the creative challenge that you want to take on for yourself?

Identifying the value that a design project can give you is a fantastic method to change *any* task into an exciting process of seeking creative solutions.

WINNER TAKES ALL

I once heard a story of a popular assignment at design schools that asks students to design a rubber-band racer. In this version of the story the students were challenged to create the fastest vehicle to cover a short distance, and they would get graded based on their speed. On race day, one of the students just took the rubber band out of her pocket, pulled it over a thumb, and launched it across the finish line. It took less than a second for the "vehicle" to cross the distance.

While it may seem that student probably missed out on the opportunity to learn how to build a racer, it is possible that everyone probably learned another important lesson—that of being able to take a step back, look at all of the variables of a given design problem, and make a conscious decision to change the problem into a different one. All of the other students were immediately focusing on trying to solve the problem that they were given, assuming that a "vehicle" needs to have wheels.

Looking at a problem from unconventional angles can lead to a path that solves the core of a problem.

One of my students tested this approach when I gave the following warm-up design exercise: develop a concept to help a company increase the sales of their paper clips. I explained that the following week we would look at who would have the best concept for our fictitious client. The results were diverse: one student did clever packaging designs showcasing all the different possible usages of paper clips, such as a "bomb diffuser;" another invented an entirely new method of holding paper together; some projects appealed to new market segments; and yet others developed concepts on how paper clips can be used for educational elementary school games. There were many more inspiring ideas, but the winning concept was from a student who did not design a paper clip. Anticipating that everyone else would have great concepts, and that the challenge would be evaluated by how much it could increase sales, the concept was the design of a storefront. The store that would eventually sell *all* of the products that the other students came up with.

I have since stopped giving this assignment.

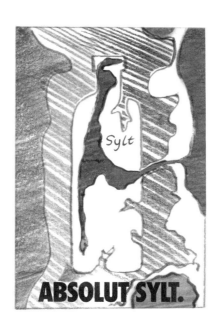

STRATEGY Nº 3: PATTERN BREAKING

Do the opposite.

One of my first encounters with pattern breaking occurred to me when I was still a teenager. It came in the form of a poster competition that I saw advertised in a magazine. The rules were to create an iconic advertising poster for my hometown of Hamburg in Germany, and it was sponsored by a well-known liquor brand. It had to specifically capture the essence of the city in a way that it would be unique and clearly recognizable. I immediately started a list of attributes that describe Hamburg, ranging from famous sights and architectural icons to typical behavioral and experiential ideas. I sorted all of the ideas into categories and felt confident that I had a great starting point. But as I looked at the rules again, I asked myself the following question:

If this competition is advertised in a magazine, how many people are going to participate?

I assumed it would be a lot of people. This triggered the second question:

How many designers will have the same criteria as I do?

Undoubtedly, most of them. It was time to break my conventional thinking in order to avoid creating a poster with a concept that someone else might have as well. After all, I wanted it to be unique and not present the same idea as someone else's. So I tried to anticipate what the other designers would focus on and try to do the opposite. The question in my mind was:

How can I represent the city without showing anything of the city?

This became at first a difficult task, because just about any visual either directly or indirectly represented Hamburg. But there was one element that I noticed in the streets of Hamburg that I knew no one else would use, because it was a symbol of a completely different place.

Hamburg is a merchant town that lies in Northern Germany, and it has a magnificent harbor. The harbor is among Europe's largest, and was once one of the main arteries of goods being delivered to all of Germany. Small waterways and bridges, which connect the various streets and alleys (it is said that Hamburg has more bridges than Venice, Italy), crisscross the city. The waterways connect to a massive lake in the heart of the city that can be used for sailing in the summer and sometimes for ice skating in the winter. It has a great music scene (the Beatles got their first start here) and is a fantastic place to grow up. Despite these rather sunny attributes, it has a weather pattern that is similar to Seattle.

The weather in Hamburg is mostly wet, and sunshine is at a premium. When it is warm and sunny, people want to go to the North Sea, with its magnificent beaches and stark landscapes. Depending on where you go, the coast is only about an hour or two away, and there are some beautiful little islands just off the shore. One of these islands is called Sylt, and it has a very distinctive silhouette. This silhouette is available as small stickers to be put onto cars, and the residents of Hamburg not only love that island they also love the stickers. They are most distinctly placed on the cars, often directly onto the license plate. It is a form of communicating to others that you are a frequent visitor of the island. I decided to make that the visual content of the poster. In essence, I was advertising the town of Hamburg with the visual of the island of Sylt.

Needless to say, my concept did not win first place. However, it won second place, and my design was soon adopted for the actual island as its iconic poster. In the case of the Sylt poster, I think that by trying to anticipate what the competition would do, I significantly changed the outcome of the design. This can have unpredictable outcomes, especially in the evaluation phase of any given project. In my case, I did not technically follow the rules because the poster represented a different place altogether. Yet, at the same time, it had enough relevance for the jury to still award second place. I have since become fascinated with the concept of trying to distill the essence of a city, because most cities are often falsely being defined by what we can see (the "sights") and not what they really are (the experiences that they allow).

DISSECTING THE PROBLEM

Walking that fine line between concept and consequence is an important part of pattern breaking as the following two scenarios illustrate.

A Problem Lobotomy

When I was a graduate student, I wanted to constantly experiment with new approaches to avoid routine. I knew that the cost of disruptive thinking would sometimes feel like wearing a costume to a party where everyone is dressed normal. In the first scenario, I was stuck in a class that asked the students to design and create a functioning pepper grinder that we had to manufacture on the lathe using natural hard woods. While the criteria were laid out relatively clearly, I had already extensive training in wood manufacturing and wanted to push myself to do something that allowed me to learn something new.

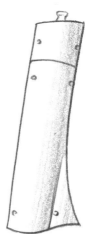

I have always wanted to use the metal CNC mill that allowed fluid shapes to be cut out of solid blocks of aluminum. By using the CNC, the design was no longer restricted to being symmetrical or cylindrical, and I took advantage of this newly found opportunity by giving the grinder a stance and posture that added character. Once the design was done, I added a brushed finish to the surface that added texture. The design was not only beautiful but also stood out from everyone else's due to the asymmetry and leaning stance. Soon there was a crowd that hovered around it, picking it up and discussing their perception of the design. I could tell that some people were not amused about the fact that I had broken the rules. Let's take a quick look at the actual criteria to understand the process:

It had to be made on the lathe.	I made it on the CNC.
It had to be made with wood.	I used aluminum.
It had to actually work.	It did.

I call this process of dissecting a problem into its individual elements a "problem lobotomy," whereby all relevant factors are looked at individually to find opportunities for pattern breaking. What is missing in the matrix above is the fact that if you use the lathe, inevitably you end up with a cylindrical and symmetrical shape. By switching the manufacturing tool to a CNC mill, my design had the opportunity to lean, which I believe was actually the biggest differentiator (and not the use of aluminum). I think if I were able to give myself a critique that day, my recommendation would have been to create two designs: one that fulfills the assignment and one that represents the ideological evolution of that concept. In either case, my instructor generously gave me a passing grade.

To become better at learning creative skills, you need to break with convention at times.

The Three-Dimensional "Poster"

Soon thereafter, I was in an academic class about Japanese art and aesthetic. For the final project, we were assigned to design a poster that had the following criteria:

- It had to feature five distinct categories.
- It had to be a comparison between East and West.
- It had to feature a combination of graphics and visuals.

Having learned an important lesson in the previous example, my question for this design problem was:

How can I break the pattern of what everyone else will produce but still follow the rules and deliver the required content?

In the process of identifying patterns, it is necessary to look at all variables—not just the ones that you are given or the ones that are in plain sight (recall this lesson from Strategy No.1: Identifying the Blind Spot). In the example of the poster, it had to contain the required deliverables, but what was not specified was what shape and form the poster would take. Thus, I decided to redefine what a poster is, or rather what it could be.

A traditional poster is two-dimensional, hangs flat on the wall, and communicates information. Immediately I knew I needed to create something that is three-dimensional and that does not hang on a wall, but it still needed to communicate. The answer came in the form of a lamp plus lamp shade (made out of a five-sided rectangle, one for each of the categories that we had to feature). The outside was printed with red ink, and I had put a red light bulb on the inside. During the presentation I turned the light on via a dimmer, which started to reveal the graphics that were printed on the inside of the lampshade with green ink (red light + green ink = black graphics). Meanwhile, the red graphics on the outside started to fade, by being illuminated by the light, giving the piece the necessary comparison of East and West. The piece was very well received, and I want to attribute this to the fact that it broke the pattern of what a poster is, while simultaneously not breaking the rules of the required content.

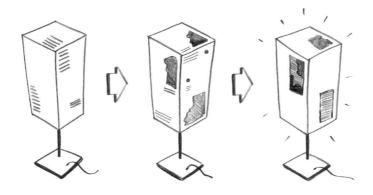

Looking at design in this way can become a fun and entertaining activity that helps to discover creative opportunities in otherwise saturated fields. It will allow you to develop concepts that solve problems that are determined by you, based on criteria that are established by yourself.

Any design problem can be dissected into criteria, and seeking and breaking these patterns is one way to challenge yourself— even though the project itself may not look like a challenge at all.

Yet many designers I know prefer to be reactive to a project, and their work becomes predictable, lifeless, and flows in the river of sameness. Don't get me wrong, the designs are still professionally executed and deserve to be recognized as being good solutions. But they are often not great, because they lack that element of unpredictability.

I like pattern breaking a lot, because it is relatively easy to do in principal, yet very challenging to pull off if you want the design to maintain a certain harmony and balance. When you take risks and are about to break the rules, always remember to look at all variables, including all stakeholders, and ask yourself how you want your work to be perceived. This can be helpful in preventing your concept from being offensive to those around you. I admit, the outcomes are not always positive, as my two examples have hopefully illustrated.

TAKE CREATIVE RISKS

There is a famous urban myth that took place in a philosophy class where the teacher gave the following question as the topic of an exam: What is courage? While everyone was busy starting with his or her analysis, one student just stared at the paper for a moment and then wrote the following sentence: "This is courage." They then handed the exam to the teacher and left. I like to think that this student deserved an A. There are a few variations of this story, but I like this one because of the *courage* needed to break the rules.

I need to make a small but very important disclaimer here: there is a difference between laws that make our society function (such as following traffic laws) and rules that guide us through our own individual cultural society (such as proper traffic etiquette). Laws are written down; rules are implied by society. Breaking laws has serious consequences, while breaking rules can get you grounded.

The laws that govern us are written down and are mostly verified by all members of society. Rules, however, are only perceived, and it is sometimes not quite clear to me where they came from in the first place. Especially in academic institutions I sometimes wonder why certain things are the way they are. I find that most rules are created by people who are no longer relevant, and it is worth questioning if their rules still apply. Breaking rules is about going beyond preconceived notions of what we think is "okay," as long as we understand the scope of possible consequences.

Try to fail.

I once had a student who was producing very consistently good work. Good, as in "B"-quality work. During one of the crits I kept silent to figure out how to improve the work. The student became very nervous and asked me what was wrong with the work. I gave the student the following advice:

"You know, there is nothing wrong with your work, and that is a problem. Your work is too safe; make it riskier."

With a disappointed look, the student responded: "But I tried so hard to get it right; I don't think I can push any further."

I realized that the student probably stayed up all night trying very hard to get the concept "right" without ever realizing what "right" actually means. I asked the student: "Have you ever tried to push a concept to the point where it goes too far, where it goes over the horizon?"

"Well, I did not want to fail the assignment . . ."

I realized at that moment that while grades are necessary, they can have an adverse effect on a designer's ability to push boundaries. While the student was trying very hard to create "great" or "A"-quality work, the reality was that the student was reaching "good," or "B"-quality work. This is a matter of not setting the goals high enough to actually reach them. For example, in training for any physical activity, you would set goals on a regular basis that are slightly out of your reach. Instead of running the mile in eight minutes, you might try to go for seven minutes next; or instead of running one mile, you might want to reach two. We are very well equipped to physically handle this kind of method of pushing our body to improve. The same principle applies to pushing your creative muscle in learning creative capabilities. The only problem is that if you want to achieve "A"-level work, you would need to set a goal on the grading scale that is beyond that. And there currently is none.

Grades in every Western society are on a scale that has a top and a bottom. I think that if you were to take a math exam and solve every problem correctly and cohesively, you would deserve to receive that top grade because you followed the math laws and showed adequate comprehension. In the creative field, however, following the rules perfectly means you are not trying hard enough to fail.

"Trying to fail" does not mean not showing up. Trying to fail means trying to have the quality of your work reach the level that is beyond an A+. It means breaking with convention and finding out what it feels like to go *too* far.

Each concept or idea that you create will receive a crit, and that evaluation can be either objective (such as the math exam) or subjective (such as a design). I have found that most people agree on what constitutes "average" and "good," and to some degree, even "great." But when a concept reaches further on that scale, all of a sudden the opinions can split drastically. Some call a design "excellent," others call it a "failure." Because of that I sometimes imagine that grades are not linear: they actually rest on a closed loop, with "A" and "F" sharing a common boundary.

THE IMPORTANCE OF "CRIT CULTURE"

ArtCenter is an amazing place and I feel humbled that I am allowed to teach there. I really have no qualifications to be a teacher. Good thing I am not alone. I can't think of any of my colleagues having any formal training in education. What makes this place so unique is that we don't have professional teachers but rather teaching professionals. The entire faculty is doing something outside of school—most teach just one or two classes—and have another career as their main focus in life. It is their expert perspectives that they bring to the classroom and to the dreaded critique process. What makes ArtCenter so enriching is a culture that cultivates crits.

Crits drive everything. Not a single project can be creative without receiving some form of a crit. These crits come from teachers, clients, alumni, and classmates. But also friends, roommates, consumers, and spouses chime in. Any feedback is taken into consideration, and the projects are revised accordingly. Some crits are more important than others, and sometimes crits happen in the hallways, over lunch, or even in the parking lot.

Established professionals in the industry also actively seek critiques regularly as part of their process to improve. This may not always be apparent, but consider the following scenario: think of professional athletes, past or present, who have reached the top tier of their disciplines; perhaps they are even the best in the world at what they do. As with any skill, they got there by practicing relentlessly. They spent the necessary time and effort to improve their skills through continuous trial and error. And they all have one thing in common: a coach.

Now if you are the best in the world at what you do, do you really need a coach? Athletes will gladly tell you that their coaches got them to where they are and help them to *stay* where they are. And not just individual athletes but also teams. If a soccer team continuously loses, they do not replace the players, they replace the coach. It is the coach who provides the critiques and helps advance the relative skill level. And this concept translates even beyond sports. Every accomplished creative has a coach-like person who helped them along the way, who provided the crits needed to succeed. This may not be apparent on the surface, but if you dig deep enough, you will always find this pattern.

These creative coaches have labels: teachers, mentors, partners-in-crime, right-hand woman or man, significant others, tutors, sidekicks, siblings, coworkers, colleagues, parents, classmates, and family members. What they have in common is that they can provide the necessary crit culture to continuously evaluate your work and progress.

Crits can provide these critical junctures where a project goes from good to great, and all the way to amazing. They can also provide creative intervention to give an objective view on how a project can be saved or steered in a different direction. Absence of these crits only leaves self-judgment in the decision-making process. It is called creating in a vacuum and rarely produces creative results.

If you want to improve the quality of your work, actively seek critiques. If you pour a lot of energy into your work and it is not progressing, find a (new) coach. Stay away from people who only tell you what you want to hear. Find those who tell you what you need to hear.

Make it an obsession to receive crits. If your work environment is isolated, get out. Actually, if you have to work in a cubicle, break the wall or look for a new job altogether. Find a space that has a crit culture, and your work will flourish.

It can be scary to be constantly evaluated. This is where fear of failure comes into play. It is the kryptonite of creativity and comes in different shades: fear of receiving a negative crit, fear of not finishing, fear of running out of resources, fear of not finding a solution, you get the idea. Nobody likes to fail or to be seen as a failure, and I am no different. When I fail, I use that moment as a stepping-stone and not a final destination. Fear of failure is certainly a strong roadblock in trying to develop new ideas. When I analyze any of my (many) failed concepts, I have always used them as an opportunity to learn something new.

I often ask:

What is the worst that can happen?

In most cases, either while still in school or working professionally, the worst that can happen is that you learn something, and that does not sound so bad after all.

A RED THREAD STORY

When my friends and I started our boutique consultancy Red Thread, we had no real clue on how to run a business. I actually still don't know how to do that. The lack of organizational structure was probably the best thing that could happen to us. And we did get rich—not financially but creatively. We had an open floor plan that allowed us to critique our work at any time in the process. There certainly was no special meeting room. The whole creative process resembled an active workshop. Our different viewpoints helped drive each of the varied projects into unchartered territories. This was made possible with mutual trust—trust that our opinions matter and that we were trying to advance our concepts instead of stagnating them.

Red Thread had two distinct meanings for us: 1) the common thread of a storyline and 2) the string that you would use to help navigate through a labyrinth. The idea here is simply that if you get lost and need to take an alternative route, you could track back your path with the use of the string. Once you would arrive at the previous intersection, you could try an alternative route to find the exit. Simply put, the red thread is a lifeline to navigate complex challenges and moments of failure.

Hired to Fail

I remember the first large project that we received when we started our design consultancy, only a few months out of school. A big advertising company out of New York hired us to develop high-level concepts for one of the brands that they represented. Simply put, the task was to produce concepts that would help the brand regain relevance in a changing market environment. There were already three other established design companies working on the same project, all of them hired by the same ad agency. A lot was at stake because the company with the best ideas would be awarded a contract to turn them into reality. We did not win. Actually I found out later that we were hired with the specific intention *not* to win.

After the final presentation of the project, I had a chance to chat with the representative from the agency to find out how we could have avoided losing to the other teams. He told me that we did everything he had hoped for and more. I had to ask:

"If we were so great, how come we didn't win?"

"Your ideas and concepts were so far out there that there is no way our client would go for any of them."

"Why didn't you tell us? We could have developed safer concepts . . ."

"I didn't hire you guys to create safe ideas; I hired you guys to help the other companies take more risks."

He went on to tell me that they specifically hired us because we had nothing to lose. He saw the creative energy in our work and intuitively knew that our ideas would be completely over the top, so he hired us to help push the conceptual development of the *other* companies further—beyond the expected. He thought that if the other (established) designers would see our concepts, it would make them feel more comfortable to see just how far an idea can be "out there." In essence we were brought in as creative catalysts and felt honored to be part of that project.

As much as I love good questions, by far my favorite one is: *what if?* It is so profoundly innocent, yet has all the potential to change the world. It works on large problems and small ones; it can help to break patterns and stimulate progress. When I am working with corporate clients, I am often told how much they love the "what if?"

process. I believe it helps them to feel free and optimistic, without constantly being told: "No, you cannot do this." I find that sometimes a good "what if?" can be a great excuse to use a childlike mindset when creating concepts, especially if you are using humor.

I like concepts that trigger a smile and make people laugh, which can be challenging, depending on what your sense of humor is. I think Germans in general overdose on irony and sarcasm. I am not sure where that comes from, but I have noticed that we practice it on a daily basis like a national obsession. One of the many ways this manifests itself in daily spoken language is that one would proclaim the exact opposite of what they mean, often with great emphasis. "It sure is sunny today" during the year-round rainy season. While I noticed that this could get somewhat annoying and confusing for my non-German friends, the concept of actively looking for opposites is actually a great method for discovering and breaking patterns.

By looking at opposites and extremes, you can discover a lot of otherwise overlooked areas for creative exploration.

I have made it a habit to always start a design project by thinking about what it is *not*—to find its opposite extreme. For example, I was once working on a design using a traditional letterpress. It is a relatively straightforward process using amazing analog technology that can create beautiful results. After gaining a solid understanding of what can be done with it, I immediately tried to find the extremes by finding out what can't be done easily. I asked a colleague of mine (who is an excellent typographer and an expert in letterpress):

"What is the letterpress machine designed not to do?"

"Well, for one, it is not designed for type to flow freely."

Which naturally made me want to experiment exactly with that challenge:

What if I have type flow organically?

This resulted in a wonderful quest to break the very pattern for which the letterpress machines were designed to provide solutions for. In this case, it was easy to experiment with this question because the machine would give physical results. In other situations, the process is completely hypothetical. For example, our school is located near NASA's Jet Propulsion Laboratory in Pasadena, and I am fascinated by all the space missions that they launch. Recently, of course, their emphasis has been to send rovers to Mars that do all sorts of testing of the surface. One of the big questions is if there ever has been water on Mars, and perhaps if there is still any left underneath the visible surface. Further, they are now working on missions that will be able to not only take samples of the soil but to also bring them back to Earth. In my mind, I couldn't help but think what would happen if they were actually able to bring water to Earth. If it were possible, it would be a very small amount, and it would be priceless. As a designer who appreciates impossible scenarios, I had to ask myself:

What if they would sell it in a bottle?

In other words, it would make a fantastic packaging design challenge to contain a priceless artifact (water from Mars), even though it is readily available everywhere on Earth for free. What would that packaging design look like? The design would hopefully be a reminder to us earthlings to not only conserve water but perhaps also to stop shipping it around the world from distances that seem like another planet, when it is readily available everywhere.

As a designer you can use this approach with just about every project; for example, one of my students was working with properties of concrete for a public-park installation. Once cured, concrete is, of course, very solid, and so the opposite became:

What if I create a design that is flexible?

This resulted in a series of experiments to give concrete flexible properties. Another student wanted to create a line of new toys and discovered the capacity that children have to use ordinary objects in a manner that they are not intended for. The project started by looking at the opposite of creating new products by asking:

What if I design existing packaging to become toys that empower children to discover the world around them?

Appropriately he designed a series of toys out of cardboard boxes.

This type of thinking has helped many students to find approaches to design problems that otherwise would have been left uncovered.

 Asking "What if?" allows for doing things differently, and is not just limited to the concept but also the development and execution of an idea.

This can be a transfer of mediums or working with mediums that you are not familiar with. As with any new or familiar medium, ask yourself what can be done with it, and more importantly, what is the opposite:

What can't be done with it—and what if you do just that?

Thinking about opposites helps in finding extremes, and I believe that is an important ingredient for innovation. Some of the great design solutions that surround us are the result of identifying what others (the competition) are not doing, or which market they are not serving. Successful designs that reach these markets often have no competition, because they break the pattern.

 As a designer, you have the opportunity to not only find alternate solutions but to redefine what constitutes a solution in the first place.

Pattern breaking is at the core of this process that can lead to groundbreaking innovative design solutions, as well as stimulating conceptual pieces. But regardless of how far out an idea is, it will remain an idea unless you proceed in making it a reality. In my mind, only then does the idea become an act of creativity.

PLANTING LIMITS

Use less.

In the famous movie *Apollo 13*, directed by Ron Howard and starring Tom Hanks, there is a powerful scene that exemplifies what a creative designer does on a regular basis. In that scene, the damaged spaceship is already on its way home, but there is not enough oxygen available for the astronauts to survive the duration of the journey. There was too much buildup of carbon dioxide, which would have eventually made the air unbreathable for the astronauts. Their only hope was to use canisters filled with lithium hydroxide, which is designed to remove carbon dioxide from the air and filter it to make it breathable. The good news was that they had plenty of the canisters—the bad news was that they could not use any of them.

Apollo 13 had two main modules: one to land on the moon, called the Lunar Module (LM); the other, to orbit around it, called the Command Module (CM). The problem the astronauts were facing was that the cube-shaped canisters that they had were designed for the CM, but they needed to make them fit into the cylindrical sockets of the LM. In other words, it was a classic square peg in a round hole kind of problem. At that point a group of scientists back at NASA got the urgent task to come up with a solution. They immediately got to work by gathering all of the parts that were known to be available on the spaceship. They spread them out on a big table and collectively developed a solution *using only what they had available*. Their makeshift device was later dubbed the "mailbox" by the astronauts, and helped in their safe return to Earth.

This is a great scene for two reasons. First, there was an immense pressure to come up with a solution in a limited time frame. They had no choice but to come through. This was *focused designing* at its best. Second, they had to solve the problem using only the tools that were available to them. They had to make do with what they had, and they did. It was the ultimate example of how powerful limitations can be in the process of solving problems. When I saw the scene for the first time, it reminded me of what I had experienced when the opposite is true, when there are unlimited resources available.

RESOURCE OVERLOAD

Before I studied industrial design in America, I used to work as an intern for a commercial production company in Germany. My unofficial title was the "runner," which describes my responsibilities with surprising accuracy. I got to experience all aspects of the production, constantly running errands left and right. It was a magical time of learning everything about the process of creating mini stories on film, where so much time, energy, and money went into perfecting every little detail to the highest possible level of craftsmanship. I learned the importance of quality and perfection because delivering anything that was just "good enough" was not an option. The most valuable insight for me though was that you cannot buy creativity. If you have virtually unlimited resources available, it can guarantee that the end result is perfectly executed (the craft), but it has absolutely no influence on the quality of the concept (the creativity).

I think there were too many creatives involved in the process: the advertising agency develops concepts for one of their clients, such as a car company or chocolate manufacturer. Once the client likes the idea, that concept is presented to production companies to bid on. Each of these production companies has a talented roster of producers, directors, and cameramen who they select for the job and create a bid. This part pretty much resembles gambling. The bid needs to be high enough to cover the hypothetical production cost, but obviously cannot be too inflated. To plan for the unknown, the budget would have a certain percentage reserved for contingency items. Just in case. Eventually the client, the agency, and the production company reach an agreement to go ahead and produce the commercial often at the cost of a sizable home.

During the preproduction phase, the original idea undergoes a series of changes where all of the stakeholders try to refine the concept into what they think is the "right" version. The client only wants to see their product featured; the agency tries to preserve the original idea, while the director wants to make it a piece of art. The result is creative chaos; too many forces pulling on a concept make it weak. The outcome is a commercial that is well executed but not memorable. The reason is simple: too many creative visions with too many resources to accomplish them.

I once asked one of the directors who I worked with how he got into the

---

business. I was interested in how one becomes a director in the first place, knowing that there are so many stakeholders and so much pressure to make an amazing product. He told me that he started out by making a "spec" commercial. ("Spec" is short for speculation, meaning the work is done out-of-pocket with the hope that it will generate interest and future opportunities). Using only what he had available, he shot the piece with his Super 8 camera. The result was grainy, full of handheld motion, and had no dialogue, only music. At the time there was no other commercial that conveyed such an authentic and unique feeling, while being honest in the use of the medium. It was the complete lack of resources that made the film stand out.

 If the idea is good, then the initial level of execution is irrelevant.

My brother, who was then a managing director at the company, told me that when looking at reels from film students, he is not looking at how professionally the spots are executed but rather how well the concept is translated. His reasoning is that the initial concept does not get better with a higher production quality.

I recently came across another spec commercial done for an airline company that was created by my cousin, who is an accomplished cameraman in Germany. I used the opportunity to ask him how he made it. He told me that he just put some personal footage together and weaved it into a story about a long-distance relationship. One particular scene caught my attention: the camera pans over the night city with a slow and steady motion, as if we are flying over it.

I asked him, "How did you shoot this? Did you rent a helicopter?"

He laughed and said, "No, I shot it from the Ferris wheel that was in town that week . . ."

He used only what he had available at the time. No special effects, no budget, only what reality had to offer.

WHEN LESS IS MORE

As part of running Red Thread, we regularly took time to fuel up on inspiration. For one of these *inspirational investment* trips (more on this in Strategy No. 6: Refueling on Inspiration), I went with our director/photographer on a journey to experience the culture of Japan. To save money we stayed at a friend's apartment, which we pretty much filled up with our suitcases, sleeping bags, and video gear. We wanted to be prepared for anything. If our presence wasn't enough trouble already, our host was gracious enough to show us some hidden treasures of Tokyo, and also took us for a weekend trip to a nearby hot spring. These natural hot springs are fueled by geothermal sources and are near-boiling temperature. As we were relaxing in the hot water, my director asked me a question:

"Hey Frido, what if we shoot a short film when we get back to Tokyo?"

It was a great question, but I was not sure if he was serious. To put things in perspective, as a foreigner who does not speak the language, it can be a bit of a challenge to accomplish anything beyond ordering a cup of coffee in Japan. Of course, Tokyo is an extremely metropolitan city, but to go out and shoot a short film did seem daunting. I said:

"Are you sure the water is not too hot for you?"

"[laughing] . . . No, I think we could do it. We have a digital camera and we can work out a story over dinner . . ."

". . . and think of locations to shoot. I could ask my friend if he knows someone that could be our actor . . ."

". . . maybe he can also help with the production?"

"Perfect, let's do it."

And we did. We developed a simple story about the difficulty of finding love in a city that is filled with so many people. My friend ended up helping us to find two suitable actors, and once we were back in Tokyo, we got to work. We had close to 10 locations that we shot at in the course of one day, all without a permit. When we saw unforeseen elements that could enrich the underlying storyline, we went for it, building and revising the script as the events unfolded. Any obstacle ("We have to wait for the next train") became an opportunity ("What if we shoot a scene here at the station while we wait?"). At some point we even found a photo booth on the street and incorporated it into the storyline. The constraints were powerful.

 Not having any resources made us use what we had in more creative ways.

My friend's apartment became one of the scenes, and so did the public botanical gardens. We figured that as long as we looked like tourists shooting tourist attractions, we would be okay. In that spirit, we concluded the film in a crowd scene at Shibuya crossing, one of the busiest intersections in all of Tokyo. On film it looked like we had about a thousand extras.

Back in Los Angeles we edited the film, and while looking for a suitable soundtrack, we came across a music-video competition. We did not intend to shoot a music video, but the song fit almost perfectly. Strange things happen when you are having fun. We submitted our short film together with the song, and ended up winning the competition. The video we shot during our vacation with no budget became the official music video for DJ Sasha, an international icon in the electronic music scene. I believe it was both the vision and story of our director and the producer that made it a winner.

MINIMUM TOOLS, MAXIMUM PAYOFF

In learning to be more creative, it helps to be organized to a certain degree—and then to allow for a form of planned spontaneity that makes the process so incredibly rewarding. What I have noticed is that more resources do not create better results; they can actually prevent creative thinking. Resources, of course, represent everything that you work with: time and tools.

When students ask for more time to complete their projects, I tell them the story of one of my students who had fractured his wrist in a bike accident. His right arm was to be in a cast and sling for two months, and unfortunately he was right-handed. He could have taken a leave of absence and retaken the class, but instead he asked me, "I want to be able to finish my project for your class. What can I do to further develop my concept and design?"

He was unable to use his right hand for drawing, cutting, gluing, lifting, or any other activity that he would need to develop prototypes of his design. For the homework, he actually tried to do the drawings with his left hand, and I admire that attempt, even though I could not recognize anything on the paper. The key for this class though was to develop a concept into a functioning prototype, and not necessarily through drawing. So I asked him, "Do you still have your LEGO?"

He did, and we decided he would use them to do the homework assignments and to develop his ideas. LEGO do not require glue, can be put together (almost) single-handedly, and most importantly, they are fast in creating prototypes. Despite the fact that my student had only one arm to design with (and on top of that his left one), he came through and finished the design. By the time his cast came off, he was ready to create a full-scale concept model of his design because he had used what could be perceived as a disadvantage, and made it into the core of both his aesthetic and functional development. And for that, he only used minimal tools, which actually made the design process *faster* for him.

GERMAN EFFECTIVENESS

When I ask my students, "When do you know that your design is done?" I get answers ranging from: "It is done when it is due" to "Never." As a designer, it is really easy to get carried away with a project and to passionately work on it—without really knowing what you are actually working on.

Whenever this happens to me, and it does happen to everyone, I try to take a moment to define what the desirable point of my project is, meaning what it actually needs to *accomplish*. I learned this in a surf shop when I was looking for a board to buy. There were too many options to choose from, so I asked for help. It turns out that the person I asked was actually one of the boardmakers. He sized me up and asked about my experience level (none), and then pulled out a special, seven-foot-long beginner board. I asked, "Why do I need this long board; can't I buy one of the cool, small ones?"

I was under the impression that the smaller boards would give more flexibility, be easier to transport, and would make me look less like an idiot who is trying to learn how to surf. I wanted to successfully accomplish surfing, and I thought a small board would get me there quicker. The boardmaker smiled and said: "With the small one, you will never learn how to stand up, because it moves too fast. But you need to be able to stand up if you want to learn how to surf. Get the long board until you know what you are doing."

You have to be able to walk in order to run.

I understood that my only priority should be to accomplish standing, not surfing. He wanted me to learn (and fail) within controlled circumstances, and the most basic tool would get me there quicker because I would learn faster.

My students often believe that with me being German, I possess some secret skill that allows me to have a higher level of productivity. They ask:

"Frido, can you show us how to apply some of your German efficiency into our work flow?"

To which I answer:

"We Germans do not try to be efficient; we actually strive for effectiveness. If we are efficient, it is only a happy accident of trying to be effective."

Working effectively means you fine-tune your project to a point where it reaches a level of beautiful simplicity in both form and function. I describe these projects as having "lean concepts," where there is no extra fat to make them more appealing. I have found it extremely valuable to establish clear guidelines as to what the design concept needs to accomplish. At the start of a project I ask:

What does the design need to accomplish in order to be successful?

The answer gives me a framework that I can use to start the design process. It is tempting to add unnecessary things to an otherwise beautiful concept.

This process helps in distilling your design down to its essence and helps in recognizing the point when your project is finished.

Keep projects as simple as possible and focus on what they need to communicate.

I found that sometimes choices that come from self-imposed constraints yield unexpected, and often better, results. For example, vehicle designs that were developed using paper prototypes will inherently look different than those using the computer. Many design solutions that I have worked on were an accidental result of a self-imposed limitation. Beyond the choice of materials (using only paper, primary colors, one brush, natural light, etc.), you can also use limitations on other resources that are less obvious (using no software, using only stock images, using no actors, using only scissors, using only one sheet, etc.), all the way to methodology limitations (using irony, using *wabi-sabi*, using philosophy, using a new style, using a new skill, etc.).

Building these kinds of frameworks around design tasks can greatly increase the quality of your creative output. The key is to create these limitations by yourself, based on your own preference, based on what your design intuition tells you. These anchors can be based on multiple aspects related to anything from inspiration to materials to performance. The choices that you make can have an amazing influence on the outcome of the design.

You need next to nothing to start the process of developing concepts, as long as you have a method to get them out of your head into a different medium. This applies to any art- and design-related field; basically pencil and paper are enough to get started. Even the greatest film is only as good as its storyboards. I have seen inspiring designs done on napkins and amazing prototypes made out of waste material. It does not matter what material you use, a great idea will always hold true to what it is, regardless of medium. Things only change when you want to take an idea to the next level.

When it comes to executing a design, a concept, or project, use the best tools that are available to make sure that nothing distracts from the main element: your idea!

Think about it. If you were a sushi chef, would you work with a plastic knife? If you were climbing a mountain, would you use a glue gun to attach anchors? If you were a firefighter, would you use a water gun? Of course not; it would not get the job done right. As a designer, it is no different: use professional tools to get the job done—right.

This does not mean that you need to get to the closest art supply store and purchase the most expensive set of tools available; pick those only after you know that you actually need them. I made the mistake when I first started my training that I actually bought everything that the class supply lists suggested. There were full sets of colored pencils and markers, all sorts of rulers and guides, brushes and paints, carving and cutting tools, and some expensive electronic toys. I hardly used any of them. Borrow from others until you have tried and tested the tools and know exactly what you need—and more importantly, know that you will need it a lot in the future (aka don't buy a letterpress machine just to make your business cards). When you know what type of tool you need, get the top of the line and use it. These tools will become your trusted partners, and you will learn how to use them to create perfection.

In addition to your tools, I found it extremely useful to have basic materials around the studio that can help facilitate the idea generation: wood, paper, glue, wire, dowels, screws, magnets, zip ties, and also unusual elements, such as found objects, miniatures, googly eyes, pop-up cards, etc. If neatly organized, these materials do not take up a whole lot of space (very important), and will be ready when you least expect it. This was the case, for example, when I quickly needed to make a prototype of a watch, and I had an old one ready for use.

 Generally speaking, using materials and products in unintended ways is a key staple to stumbling across new ideas, but it only works if you have these things around you when you are working.

For that purpose, I regularly collect objects, materials, and artifacts that I want to use for future projects. They are neatly organized so that I can find them again, and most importantly, I regularly go through them to sort out what I no longer need. That way the collection does not get out of control and remains useful.

FAIL-FAST PROTOTYPING

Test, iterate, repeat.

A long time ago, in a land far away, there once was an emperor who had a rooster. This rooster was his pride and joy, and he set out to find the best artist in the country to commission a painting of the animal. Once the artist was found, he got invited to the court to meet with the emperor—and the rooster. The artist felt honored and thanked the emperor for entrusting him with such an important piece of art. He said he would begin right away and returned back to his studio that was located in a small village by the sea.

When a month went by without any word from the artist, the emperor sent a messenger to inquire about the painting's progress. The messenger returned and reported that the artist was not done yet. Another month went by and again the emperor sent a messenger, and again he returned to report that the artist was still working on the painting. This went on for three months, six months, one year, and the response was always the same: the painting is not done yet.

The story goes that finally after two years, the messenger came back to the emperor with the good news: the rooster painting is done! The emperor was so thrilled that he decided to pick it up in person and embarked on a journey to the artist's studio. As he and his delegation arrived in the small seaside town, they made their way to the humble studio of the artist who welcomed them inside. Once they all took a seat and had tea, the emperor asked impatiently to see the painting. The artist took a blank canvas and a brush, and with a few swift strokes, created a beautiful painting of the rooster.

The emperor was both impressed and stunned at what he saw. He asked a simple yet poignant question: "Why did you have me wait for two years if it only takes you a few moments to create the painting?"

The artist bowed deeply and apologized, asking for forgiveness. He then opened a door that led to huge a storage room. That room was filled from floor to ceiling with paintings of the rooster. He had spent the last two years practicing his craft before he was ready to create the final product. What looked like the result of a few moments, actually took two years to perfect. What looked like an easy task was the result of continuous prototyping and iterating.

START BY DOING

As with any tale, there are variations of this story that have different time frames and also feature different animals, but the essence remains the same: in order to accomplish anything, you need to start by making. I love this story because I feel that it describes a very important aspect of the creative process that I have learned to trust blindly:

Solutions are out there—it is just a matter of trial and error to find them.

And with that in mind, I try to start as quickly as possible. I don't try to find the right solution, the one that works. That one will present itself automatically. I am trying as quickly as possible to eliminate all of the wrong solutions.

This process of trial and error is a form of prototyping. In this context, a prototype is just an expression of a possible solution that is ready to be evaluated with a crit. It is a material that is tested for performance, an idea that is shared with a friend for feedback, or a drawing turned upside down to check for composition and perspective. In the rooster story, each one of the paintings that the artist created was a form of a failed attempt that was necessary to improve the skill and get closer to the actual solution. In the end, the final product of this process looks easy, and that is the beauty of it.

The process of exploration through prototyping is like a race of testing results constantly to see if it "works." Inevitably things happen that are unplanned (both good and bad) and result in moments of serendipity. These "aha" moments can lead to solutions that otherwise would have not been possible. One classic example of this is the invention of the Post-it Note. A 3M scientist, Spencer Silver, was working on developing a super-strong adhesive and accidentally created a low-tack adhesive instead. The leadership did not see any usefulness in this product and did not develop it further (to them, it was not solving any problems). A few years later, his colleague by the name of Art Fry used the adhesive to create a bookmark. The now famous canary-yellow color was the result of using yellow scrap paper (it was the only kind available in the lab at the time). Elements of chance should sometimes be embraced.

Unless you are working on something, accidents cannot happen in the first place.

I feel that in the field of design, these moments of happy accidents push the original design intent in unexpected directions, often improving the final result tremendously. In contrast, when working on a design solution without iteration, the result can still be creative, but tends to be more predictable. I often see students that decide early on in the design process what they want (a combination of a function and an aesthetic) and then spend all of their time on refining their design, without ever exploring or testing different options. The result will be a good design, but not necessarily a great one.

On the other hand, I noticed that when students start right away with prototyping multiple ideas, they consistently reach more creative design solutions. Failing early and failing often (and learning from the results) produces better projects. This is one of the few principles that I believe is universally true across all creative disciplines and all fabrics of life. There is even mathematical proof for this, and it comes in the unlikely form of dissecting a game show.

When I first heard this story, I was in disbelief and had to check the facts. It is called the Monty Hall Problem (named after the host of the show *Let's Make a Deal*), and it goes like this: Imagine you are a contestant in a game show, and there are three doors to choose from. One of them contains a prize and two of them contain nothing. You get to pick one of the doors in the hopes that it has a prize behind it. Your chances are one in three. The game show host now opens one of the doors that you did not pick. It has nothing behind it. Now there are two doors left, one that has the prize and one that has nothing. You then get a chance to switch from your original choice to the other remaining one. Would you do it?

Amazingly, if you were to switch, you would actually improve your chances of winning a prize, and it is based on mathematics. When you first pick a door (Door A), the odds are one in three, or 33 percent, or *three* options. However, once the host opens one of the doors (say Door C), and reveals there is no prize behind it, you can increase your odds of winning, but *only* if you switch. How can that be? Even though Door C was revealed to have no prize, if you stick with your original choice, then the initial 33 percent odds will remain regardless of this new information, because your choice is still based on where you started, with *three* choices. But if you *switch* to Door B after the host has revealed Door C has no prize, your odds increase to two in three or 66 percent, because that choice is informed by the fact that you know one out of the three choices (Door C) has no prize behind it. There is now a 2/3 probability of a favorable outcome, you choosing the "prized" door. There is still no guarantee to win, but a lot better odds than your first pick (Door A) out of three choices, and even better odds than if you had started the game show with a choice between two doors, which would have odds of a one out of two favorable outcome, or 50 percent.

Interestingly enough, even PhD-degree holders sometimes disagree with this rationale until they are shown computer simulations (and even then they dispute reality). In comparison, if pigeons are put to the same test, they *very* quickly learn to switch.

It is helpful to apply a similar mathematical principle of probability to the creative process: the more often you switch (iterate) your idea, the closer you get to the "prize" (better solution). You have to start by making a first (blind) guess toward a solution, and then keep making new choices as new information becomes available from your prototypes (similar to the reveal of another door). If you stick with your first idea, the odds are against you, especially if there are many doors ahead of you. Creatives know this intuitively and use this to advance their projects consistently. For someone who is at the very start of her or his career, this can be a daunting task though: how many doors (failures) do you need to eliminate before you get to the solution? Many, for sure. You may as well get started with the process.

 It does require relentless energy and courage to go through this process of purposely failing, but it is also one of the most rewarding learning experiences to participate in.

THE CASE OF THE NAPKIN SKETCHBOOK

One fine evening, I was at a bar having a few beers with a friend of mine who loves to sketch. The discussion ranged from design, dinosaurs, and friendship all the way to the meaning of life (recall the number 42 from Strategy No.1). While the latter part of the conversation did not yield any results that are worth recounting, we did cover a lot of ground on projects that we were both working on. These ideas were drawn on napkins that covered the entire table when we were ready to leave. I crammed them into my pocket and wondered:

Is there a better way to carry these ideas with us?

This was a question of curiosity that was soon followed by inquiry:

Are there cases that are made to carry napkins?

I was not able to find a solution to my problem, so I went on to ask myself the question that triggers action:

What would a napkin sketchbook look like?

A short while later I found myself in some waiting room—waiting. I hate waiting. It looked like it was going to be a while so I grabbed some nearby flyers, borrowed a pen from the reception desk, and started ideating the napkin sketchbook. I love the ideation process because it allows me to dream. I ask a lot of questions and then draw possible solutions. As many as possible. I also realized that I constantly forget my pens everywhere. Through that process I distilled a new question:

How can I integrate a pen into the sketchbook?

One of the challenges of holding napkins in a sketchbook is they are loose. I wanted the sketchbook to be filled with napkins from bars and cafés and held securely when I leave. And that is when I would typically forget my pen. That led me to the next question:

What if the pen is the closing mechanism for the sketchbook?

The pen would act as a bolt, much like the hinge on a door. The sketchbook itself would act like a small tray holding the napkins in place, and they would be accessible once the pen is removed. Back in the studio I immediately made a quick cardboard mock-up. It worked and I knew the concept was done, because I saw the solution physically in front of me. However, the design process would continue, as I was about to transfer mediums.

Up until that point, I had not worked with leather, but I intuitively knew that this material was the right choice for the sketchbook. It is sturdy yet flexible, ages beautifully, and has phenomenal tactile qualities. Plus it would give the sketches that were done on disposable napkins the cozy home that they deserve. The problem was that I did not know how to fabricate a high-quality prototype that would take the essence of the cardboard version to the next level. Since I knew that I would not be able to find a "Napkin Sketchbook Manufacturer," I did the next best thing, which is to try and identify who might have the needed skills for this job. I met a handful of local craftsmen, showed them the mock-up, and asked if they could fabricate a prototype for me. The only one that wanted to give it a try was a shoemaker. The result was so bad that I almost quit.

The sketchbook closely resembled roadkill. It did not have structure because the leather was too thin. This was compensated with hand stitching on the edges that forced parts of the walls to bulge out unevenly. Worse though, the leather that was used was shiny and chocolate-colored with a very bumpy surface texture that just looked frightening. As much as the execution was a complete failure in both form and function, it gave me new ideas on what the next prototype would need. Or more precisely *who* I needed to recruit for the next prototype.

From the failed prototype I drew a few distinct conclusions:

FIRST PROTOTYPE	NEXT PROTOTYPE
Leather is weak.	Leather needs to be strong.
Leather is textured.	Leather needs to be smooth.
Leather is brown.	Leather needs to be natural.
There was uneven stitching.	Stitching needs to be part of the design.

Seeing the failed attempt gave me a clear vision of what the sketchbook should look like: a saddle.

I found an Irish master saddlemaker with a cockney accent who was nearly impossible to understand. He told me that he has been making saddles for more than 15 years, and has never had anyone request him to create a sketchbook, so he was really interested. All I heard though was "15 years of experience," which was confirmation to me that I had found the right guy. A week later he delivered a prototype that was perfect in every sense of the word. It was of better quality than I could have ever hoped for. He told me that he actually had his apprentice work on this project, and that his apprentice had to create multiple versions to get it done right. They were doing their own version of fail-fast prototyping.

 What this story illustrates is that the ideation and iteration process is key in visualizing solutions that otherwise would remain out of sight.

I needed to look at the first prototype to gain a clear insight as to what was wrong with the design. The visual crit allowed me to understand how to make it right. Seeing the same concept on paper, even with the help of a cardboard mock-up, did not prevent the design to fail when it was first translated into a new material. Without that critical failure, it would have taken me much longer to create the design, and it would have lacked the perfect execution that came with 15 years of experience.

 Any transfer of medium can have a profound impact (for better or worse) on the design development. The trick is to treat each occurrence as just another prototype and to improve it in the next round.

Remember that unless you are working on a project, nothing positive can happen. Failure is part of the process and can give clear directions for the next iteration. In the case of the napkin sketchbook, I could have spent time and energy to become a leather craftsman myself, but in this scenario it was more *effective* to outsource the work to the *right* expert.

Even the experts test their output relentlessly. The saddlemaker and his apprentice made multiple "tests" before creating the final version. Architects make countless models before building a house. Expert chefs taste every dish before serving them to guests. Great bartenders taste every drink to ensure consistent quality (at least that is what they have us believe). Go ahead and test-drive your ideas and allow for serendipity to happen.

KAIZEN

I love to paint with traditional mediums because, unlike solving a design problem, it is never entirely clear when the painting is actually done. Most designs undergo these wonderful stages of development and transfers of mediums that are exciting to observe. With painting, though, you are working with the final medium entirely. Whatever you have in front of you is already the end result. Any missing elements are merely in the tube and just need to be applied. Painting is a process that allows for constant improvement. This improvement can start right from the beginning. When I was learning how to paint, my teacher taught me to lay down a foundation covering the entire canvas. He called this the "wash." Even if some parts were left white with the canvas still showing, he still insisted on covering it with water. He would then say: "See, you are practically done; now all you need to add are the missing elements!"

It took me years to fully understand what he meant. He knew that learning the skill of painting can be daunting, especially if the first attempts end in failure.

The process of starting was the most important step, because along the way every mistake could be altered later on.

His way of teaching was to make continuous improvements to the end product. By covering the entire canvas, even with just water, the painting was practically done. In school I remember that we would work together until late into the night on our homework only to later face a rather devastating critique in the classroom. However, his famously honest crits took only a small portion of class time, the rest would be used to implement the feedback and to make our work better. At the end of class everyone showed their paintings again—and the revised versions were stunning improvements compared to what we started with.

I learned that just about anything can be altered and improved with a continuous process of revising the final product. My teacher also covered the importance of creating *comps*. A comp is a small painting that attempts to capture the essence of the concept, including the composition, color, and depth. These comps would take minutes to create (compared to hours for the final pieces), thus they were immensely valuable in our process. These comps possessed a certain energy and level of indication that strongly influenced the technique that we used for the final pieces. Translated to design, these comps were prototypes or mock-ups of the final version. Ever since then I have embraced the value of starting with the initial comp, and then making continuous improvements to it until it is finished.

This principle of continuously making something better is beautifully contained in the Japanese word *kaizen*, which refers to a specific method of working. In a way, it is not about working faster but rather improving both work conditions and the product itself through a continuous system of incremental change. Literally translated, kaizen means "continuous improvement." The Japanese have successfully implemented this method of working into the development of many of their products, such as cars and electronics. As a result, these products are far superior in function and reliability than most of their competitors.

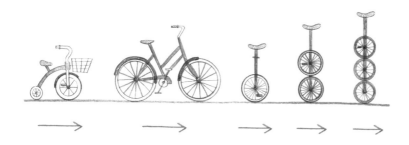

The secret to success is not really a secret at all: kaizen simply implies embracing change to improve the work.

In most Western societies, "change" is typically only accepted if handed down from above, while in the Japanese society, change is accepted unilaterally (as long as it is in small steps). Kaizen does not necessarily imply that the process of improvement should be filled with failures. Originally it is a term that describes a business working methodology and not a process in the creative field.

THE FIVE-YEAR THEORY

There are many well-known examples in the business of innovation that in essence describe a principle of continuous failure. We all have heard the famous quotes about how many attempts it took someone to finally have his or her idea manifested. What these examples often do not refer to is the element of time: about five years. While I have since read this number (and other versions) in popular books, I actually got it from a conversation that I had with a colleague and friend of mine about how long it takes to become an expert in any given aspect of the design field.

His reasoning was that anyone could become great at drawing (aka expert); it just takes the necessary hours to build up the skill. He estimated it to be 10,000 hours, which is a number that seems slightly out of reach. These hours spread over normal working days and hours would roughly end up to be five years until anyone could be an expert in any given field. This is, of course, not a scientific number, but nonetheless an interesting notion to keep in mind when practicing creativity. What I liked so much about his argument was that I remembered hearing it before, during a sports report in the 1984 Olympics from Los Angeles.

During that time I was living in Germany, and Los Angeles was an unknown and faraway place. The news reporters were following all of the German athletes, but there was one in particular who captured everyone's imagination. It was Jürgen Hingsen, the West German competitor who was in one of the most demanding disciplines of the Olympics: the decathlon! In the decathlon, athletes compete in 10 different sport events, and they need to be an expert at all of them. After each competition they would receive points, and the sum of all points would determine their rankings. That lineup would change after each event, as some athletes were naturally better at some disciplines than others. Hingsen did not win, but received a well-deserved silver medal.

What stuck in my head though was one of the discussions that the reporters were having in-between events. Since the athlete caught the attention of everyone in Germany who followed the Olympics that year, they wondered how one becomes a decathlete in the first place. They had interviews with coaches, experts, and athletes. The conclusion was that as long as you start with a person who is physically capable of performing the 10 athletic disciplines, it "only" takes about five years of continuous training to compete in international sports competitions.

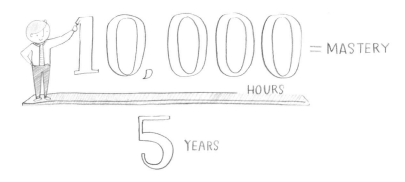

I have since found many examples in other fields where the time frame needed to become an expert follows similar patterns. Most notably is a 1993 research paper by Anders Ericsson that introduced the idea of 10,000 hours of deliberate practice—but over a period of 10 years—to reach mastery in playing the violin. (This was done by researching violinists at the Music Academy of West Berlin). He has since emphasized the importance of the role of a teacher (recall this lesson from Strategy No. 3: Crit Culture) in accelerating the path to expertise in response to many books that may have misinterpreted his research.

Perhaps not surprisingly, a typical college or university education lasts just about five years if you take internships into account. If you think about it, an internship is another prototype to test your skills in the field. It is similar to creating a small comp before diving into the process of finishing a full painting. Knowing that the process of learning is a long road, you may as well get started with the first step.

There is a famous math problem that illustrates this perfectly: if it takes five teachers one semester to teach a given skill or knowledge to a student, how many teachers would you need to teach the same content to that student in one week? Assuming a typical academic semester is 18 weeks, the mathematical answer would be: 90.

The real philosophical answer though is that it is impossible to learn that content in such a short time, no matter how many teachers you throw at the problem. Learning to be more creative is a long journey; may as well get started.

 While it is possible to increase the quality of learning from failure through expert guidance (aka teachers and coaches), it is not possible to shortcut the time and practice that it takes.

REFUELING ON INSPIRATION

Feed your mind.

How nice it would be if the concept of perpetual motion were a reality, but for now we are stuck with the laws of physics. And according to the first and second law of thermodynamics, in a closed system a machine cannot create new energy to keep itself running. The same principle can apply to the creative field. If creativity is your output, then inspiration is the input to keep the machine (which is you) running.

The term *inspiration* is often referred to as an unconscious burst of creativity. Some definitions go even further and consider it to be a spiritual or magical gift. The origin of the Latin word *spirare* is simply "to breathe." Thus inspiration in the literal sense means "the act of inhaling and exhaling"; to me it implies that we need to go outside and get a breath of fresh air to get inspired. Of course there are plenty of texts (books and articles) that describe the origins of inspiration in mythology and spiritual worlds, but it is more effective to think of inspiration as something that exists in the present, not the past. In either case, inspiration is undoubtedly linked in some way to the process of creating, both in art and design. In the context of creative strategies, inspiration is the *fuel* for creativity.

PUSHING THE RESET BUTTON

When working on design projects, I have often found myself not knowing when to stop. This is because I love what I do and can easily lose track of the world around me. I am constantly striving for perfection and make sure that all elements are fully developed to the highest possible quality level. Like any designer, I am usually not just working on one design but on multiple ones simultaneously. Projects turn into continuous streams of overlapping designs that leave no room or space to take a breath—to refuel on inspiration. If left unquestioned, I go into autopilot and my work becomes reactive and not proactive. I create designs as a reaction to a project brief without a proactive creative-strategy approach. In situations like this, I noticed that I ran out of creative fuel and needed to push my reset button: to stop everything and get out of my studio. I have learned that inspiration is not something that just comes to me like a dog that I whistle for.

 While some people believe that they need to wait until inspiration finds them somehow, you could physically go out and *get* it yourself. And opportunities for that are everywhere.

Creativity and inspiration are not only closely linked together, they are symbiotic—one is useless without the other. Realizing this unique relationship of input and output made me understand that being creative uses up a lot of energy, and that I need to invest some regular time to find sources. Stimuli like Internet research, books, and magazines for the most part only help in continuation of a project that is already in progress. But they do not necessarily facilitate completely new and original design ideas, and they do not create any energy needed to continuously produce. I realized that I needed to regularly invest time into experiencing new and unexpected things; I refer to it as time for inspirational investment.

Thanks to my creative career, I have been fortunate enough to have lived on three continents, which I believe gives me a lot of cultural references to draw from. I remember that by coming to America I actually understood my German heritage better because I had a way of comparing it. But the location that inspired me the most in my life—by far—is Tokyo. I was living there to work on a major video-game title. Living in Tokyo felt like being in the future because of the amazing architecture, advanced technology, and superb design culture. If I look at the work that I created during that time, I can now see how it was directly influenced by my surroundings. The visual of the city as a living organism was reflected in the game environments that I created. I was fascinated by the ingenious use of space, the approach to light and shadow, as well as the textures that were created by the change of seasons.

Tokyo was a fundamental game changer in my ability to see and recognize things familiar yet different. And to me, everything was completely upside down: cars drive on the "other" side of the street, language is written in unrecognizable characters, and food is served raw. All aspects of life, beyond the studio that I was working in, were entirely new. When there is no more "normal," all of a sudden everything becomes inspiration. The city allowed me to break my own thinking patterns, and thus my work was soaked with new creative fuel. It is fair to say that this city acts like a creative drug for my mind.

Inspiration can be a physical location that you visit, experience, and engage with. This can be as close as the nearest bookstore and as far as an island in Japan, thousands of miles away. Coupled with a good sense of curiosity, these locations help to put new knowledge into the brain that transforms into creative fuel at a later time.

However, it can be surprisingly difficult to make a conscious effort to break with normal work habits to get inspired on a regular basis. One of the reasons for this is that we are very comfortable with routine. We take the same route to work, we go to the same coffee shop, we watch the same television show. Unfortunately none of these activities contribute much to our personal inspirational-investment strategy.

To test this, think about what was inspiring to you over the past couple of months. I immediately think of places that I have been to that carried unique experiences. These experiences have become memories because they were different from the normal activities. I believe that when we are using inspiration we are actually mining our memories and experiences. Through that process, memories get connected and become ideas. These ideas become the fuel for creative output.

 During periods when the mind is taken off its routine, it can absorb new information, almost as if it were stocking up supplies for the winter.

FINDING PARALLEL UNIVERSES

I have always been a big fan of designs developed in the Bauhaus spirit. This is probably in part due to the fact that I grew up in Germany and that somehow the Bauhaus aesthetic has been absorbed by our culture. When I began studying industrial design, I was fascinated to learn about modernism and minimalist designs, and have subsequently tried to capture that aesthetic in my work as well. My personal design sense has been further shaped and refined by the experiences that surrounded my education and professional work. I firmly believed that if anything was to be "designed," it would need to equal modernism, and everything that did not fall within that equation was subsequently not technically "design." That aesthetic opinion of the world changed completely when I discovered a universe that existed in parallel to mine. That parallel universe is wabi-sabi.

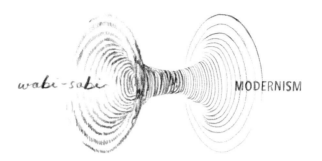

Ever since I worked in Japan, I have had a strong interest in the origins of the Japanese design aesthetic. While living in Tokyo, I was impressed not only by the futuristic and sleek architecture, and the high-tech vehicles and products, but also by the influences of traditional culture. As a city, it felt like living with one foot in the future and the other in the past. It only took one turn into a small alley or park to be transported hundreds of years into the past by seeing temples and structures that have been untouched by time and progress. I was very interested in learning more about the culture, mostly because I had a difficult time grasping it from my German point of view. When I moved from Europe to America, I remember being able to quickly draw comparisons and understand the different nuances in art and design between the two continents. In the case of Japan, it would take me almost five years (recall this lesson from Strategy No. 5: The Five-Year Theory) to discover the key that helped me make sense out of the differences. As it turns out, that key had been in plain sight all the time; it was in my blind spot.

Tea Time

As part of a design project in grad school, I was researching the origins and rituals of tea drinking. I had heard of the tea ceremony but had never paid too much attention to it up until that point. During my research I came across references to a monk named Sen Rikyu, who is credited with being one of the main pioneers of perfecting the art of the tea ceremony. What struck me, though, was a reference that as a young monk he studied the wabi-sabi aesthetic, which later influenced the design of the tea ceremony. I felt very intrigued because I had never thought of an aesthetic being applied to a process. From my Bauhaus perspective, the aesthetic was the result of the process (aka form follows function), and not the other way around. Further, I did not know what wabi-sabi really meant; in fact, I first almost wanted to mistake it for the term wasabi (which is a radish-based garnish with a very intense flavor).

Despite my intricate interest in Japanese design, I had never come across the term wabi-sabi as a way to describe an aesthetic, even though it has been around for more than 500 years. It turns out that the expression in itself can be so vague that even most Japanese people have a difficult time trying to pinpoint exactly what it means. A relatively general view of wabi-sabi is that it represents wisdom in natural simplicity and an appreciation of flawed beauty. A more detailed attempt is to specify the products of the wabi-sabi aesthetic as being irregular, impermanent, and imperfect. To me, that last word is what really made me curious, and I wondered:

How can a design be imperfect on purpose?

By digging deeper, I came across other artists who struggled with the same problem. One particular book about wabi-sabi (authored by Leonard Koren) tried to pinpoint the aesthetic by calling out what it isn't, and this was done by comparing it to modernism. The comparison showed that wabi-sabi in many ways reflects the opposite aesthetic viewpoint of modernism, and that both have a relevant place in their respective cultural traditions. Inspired by this comparison, here is a simplified version for your reference:

MODERNISM	WABI-SABI
Mass-produced for consistency	Individually made for personality
Use of natural materials to show progress	Use of natural materials to show honesty
Sleek and shiny surfaces that need to stay polished in order to look good	Surfaces that are natural and become more beautiful with use
Minimalism is achieved through engineering	Minimalism is achieved through modesty
Use of force to combine objects	Use of diplomacy to join forces
Feels cold and foreign to the touch	Feels warm and intimate through use
Nature needs to be controlled	Nature needs to be celebrated
Futuristic and meant to last (until it breaks)	Everlasting and meant to age (and then repaired)
Based on geometry and rational thought	Based on organic shapes and thought
Celebration of perfection and symmetry	Appreciation of imperfection and symmetry

In our Western worldview, wabi-sabi, in essence, represents that beloved pair of old jeans. It has marks of wear and tear, and is stitched, fixed, and repaired until it is barely recognizable as pants. It starts out as a mass-produced item but, through its use, becomes an individual and intimate friend. The irony is, of course, that many companies in the Western world would love to have their products be celebrated like a pair of jeans, but sadly, very few do. I think this is because most products are designed using primarily the left side of the chart, avoiding the right one at all costs. For my project I felt so inspired by this discovery that I used it throughout every aspect of the development of my concept.

The task was to design a tea set using bags that would afford a new tea drinking experience. In searching for examples of the wabi-sabi aesthetic, I came across the design of Ryoanji, which is a famous rock garden in the heart of Kyoto. The asymmetry and textures of the rocks became the main inspiration for the design of the cups and kettle. I created uneven shapes that were leaning toward each other—almost as if they were having a silent conversation. The handle and spout of the kettle were made out of wood, inspired by Japanese wood joinery.

In one of the prototypes (recall this lesson from Strategy No. 5: Fail-Fast Prototyping), I was playing with a circular handle and discovered that it could act as a lever to remove the tea bag from the liquid to stop the steeping process. The tea bag was thus designed to have a long string with a wooden peg that nested on the handle. When the tea was ready, the user would pull on the peg, which would lift the bag out of the liquid, eliminating the need to find a place for it on the table. The design result was unlike anything I had worked on before because I was able to use inspiration from my parallel universe as the main decision-making engine.

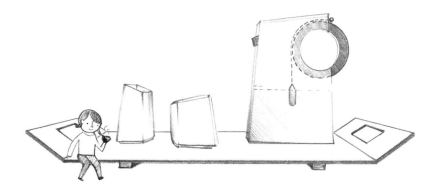

The View at the Top

Oftentimes, inspiration can be the main differentiating factor when developing concepts. This was the case when I worked on a project brief that asked for conceptual designs of small living spaces that have a higher quality of living. The premise was that with the increase of the global population, more people will likely live in dense urban areas, and current solutions often resemble windowless prisons that are depressing to live in. I knew this firsthand from living in a tiny box when I was working in Japan. From that experience, I knew that I did not necessarily need a lot more space but rather a more interesting view. I started my design process by reframing the problem:

What if everyone could live on the top floor?

The question was based on the typical multistory apartment building that I lived in. I noticed that although the place was tiny and had little natural light due to an adjacent structure, there was a spot in the building that was magical: the roof. I find that no matter how small a living space is, it is usually much more spacious once you have a bit of a view. As a result, the rent typically increases for higher floors. I wondered if it would be possible to guarantee that you could live on the top floor—at least for a while. My reasoning was that if you live in a relatively small box, it should be possible to have that box move up and down like an elevator. The problem is that if you have multiple boxes that create an apartment complex, the traditional elevator system would not work. So I chose to use a paternoster, which is an elevator that has inspired me since my childhood in Germany.

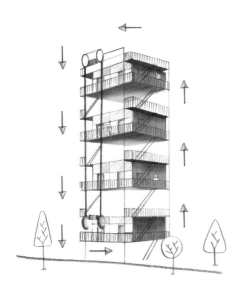

A paternoster is a strange elevator in that it is moving slowly and continuously. If you want to go up, you literally jump on a small platform that transports you higher. To exit, you jump off that same platform once you have reached the right floor. The same process applies for going down as well. As a child I loved riding these elevators, especially because I was under the impression that when your platform reaches the top, it would have to turn upside down. That was, of course, not the case, as the platforms function more like boxes that are hanging from a cable, similar to that of a ski lift. I loved riding all the way to the top only to be able to see the actual mechanism that transferred the box over to the side before descending again. And that mechanism is exactly what inspired my concept.

The final design was a four-story building with shipping container–sized apartments. Once a week the entire structure would rotate into a new hierarchy, thus everyone would get to live on the top floor at least once during the course of a month. And then the cycle would repeat. In this case study, I had two inspirational influences: living in a small box in Japan and playing with paternosters in Germany. Both were experiences that are available to anyone, as long as they seek parallel universes.

To me, parallel universes are rich sources of information that exist in plain sight but are mostly overlooked. It can be something as simple as a cultural aesthetic like wabi-sabi, or as complex as the technology in an elevator. I have found that cultures in general offer an incredible amount of inspiration for art and design. These do not even need to be far away; often a culture can also be a subculture that lives right within our "perceived" normal world—all you need to do is go to new places.

Ever since discovering this cultural strategy, I have made it a habit to listen closely to my intuition when it comes to making decisions on where to go: whether it's planned, such as deciding on a destination for an inspirational trip, or as random as making a right-hand turn to see where the road leads. I have found that it is easier to venture out on a regular basis for small "investments," because there is less pressure to find something amazing like the city of Atlantis.

inspiration

With less at stake, there is a greater chance to discover something original.

For example, just think of what you would typically do if you only had half a day to spend in a popular city, such as San Francisco or Paris. The temptation is to hit one or two of the popular sights, take some pictures, and return perhaps with a souvenir or two without much of a chance of finding inspiration.

Instead, try to shift your paradigms and values. Lower your guard just a bit and go with the flow of natural discovery. Skip the sights and seek inspiring situations contained within the environment instead. Burn your guidebook and ask the locals where to go. Actually, ask the locals if you can hang out with them. Keep a journal to document your observations, conversations, and discoveries; you never know when you will need to mine through those experiences for inspiration.

BE A SKILL SEEKER

Students often ask me about life after school as if it is some other dimension that they will enter. Specifically, they wonder what work will be like after they are done with learning. To facilitate the process, I ask them an important question:

"What do you think is the purpose of getting a design education?"

Once again, it is a simple question. So simple that it takes students a moment to see if I am joking. Once they see that I am hoping for an honest answer, they usually respond more or less with:

"To get a job . . . ?" nervously looking at me to see if they got the trivia right.

"No, if you get a job as a result, then that is a happy side effect of the education, but it is not the purpose. The purpose of the education is to make you a lifelong learner."

"Does that mean that once I graduate I am not done with learning?"

"That is true. In fact, after graduation is when the real learning begins. Design school just prepares you for how to learn effectively."

I go on to tell the student that this conversation will probably only make sense to them about a year or two after they graduate. That is roughly how long it took me to recover from being an institutionalized student and to realize that I had received the greatest gift of all: the ability to pick up skills wherever and whenever I wanted. To me it feels similar to a scene in the movie the *Matrix,* where Neo and Trinity are running away from the agents and are left on a rooftop with no escape but an Apache helicopter. The problem is that they do not know how to fly it—yet. In this awesome sci-fi movie, Trinity asks the operator in the real world to download a program so that she can learn how to fly the helicopter instantly. A few seconds later the program is complete, and they can make the daring escape. That short scene almost perfectly expresses what I learned by attending design school, which is that any skill can be acquired. Of course, we do not live in a world where we can download a skill within seconds as it is portrayed in the movie, but the point of the example is not the speed of learning but rather the possibility of being able to learn anything you want.

 This summarizes the purpose of a great education: the ability for an individual to actively acquire new skills throughout life.

Sometimes this need to learn something new actually is a prerequisite for a particular project. If you are designing for a particular sport, you better become an expert by actually participating in the sport. This develops a level of empathy that can become an empowering tool of knowledge for your design process. And only by learning the limitations, by using the equipment, and by pushing the limits, can you break away from obvious solutions.

 A hands-on approach to learning everything there is to learn about a topic will help you discover problems that have far greater solutions. That is because your design process will be fueled by personal *knowledge* of what actually makes a great concept as opposed to *guessing* that it might be a good idea.

But on the other hand, I also recommend students learn new skills that are not related to anything that they are currently working on, but that they are simply interested in. Do this proactively and regularly before you need to refuel, and you will find that your creative process remains constantly in motion. This can be as simple as reading a how-to book or attending a local workshop. Most colleges also offer evening and weekend courses on a variety of topics that can be of interest. In the process of searching for skills, I have taken classes in ceramics, screen printing, painting, photography, lithography, figure drawing, flower arrangement, paper making, and letterpress printing.

> With a regular investment in learning new skills, the mind gets constantly stimulated and challenged to think of new solutions.

There are fantastic scholarships, stipends, and grants out there that will support you in your creative efforts. All you need to do is to dig deep to find them, and apply with a meaningful proposal. Investing in your own creative future is one of the best things that you can do for yourself. Regardless of the effort invested, the inspirational rewards will always be positive.

STRATEGY Nº 7: VISION CALIBRATING

Set a new north.

My journey to becoming a teacher was a serendipitous one. About a year after graduating from ArtCenter, my alma mater called me because they needed a replacement instructor for a 3D software class. This was, of course, both a great honor and a daunting task at the same time. Even though I knew the software very well back then, I had never taught before. For the first class I tried to prepare a solid three-hour lecture to go over the various tools and workflows, as the software did not come with very cohesive instruction manuals. The software developers were very busy continuously improving many of the amazing features and, as a result, neglected to document ways on how to properly use them. I figured that I could demonstrate the functions in the classroom, and the students would be able to take notes and understand the workflow. Or so I thought.

The first day of the class I was a bit nervous and spoke for what seemed to be the entire three hours, introducing the various features and workflows. After I thought I was done and ready to give the assignment for the following session, I looked at the time, and only 20 minutes had passed! I told the students to take a break, which gave me a moment to figure out what I would do for the remaining two and a half hours. I quickly put together a simple demonstration on how the students could best tackle the first homework assignment, knowing the kind of challenges that they might face when trying to do things on their own. I was able to anticipate exactly the problems that they would run into because I had made the same mistakes myself when I was a student. They loved the demonstration and were so focused that they had a difficult time simultaneously taking notes. They asked:

"Hey, Frido, could you write us a handout for next week?"

For someone who loves a good question, this was certainly one I could easily answer; after all, it seemed like a relatively simple task. I reasoned I could use this handout every subsequent semester, so I sat down and wrote it specifically from the perspective of a student trying to use the software for the first time. Of course, what I did not anticipate then was that the following semester the new group of students got so accustomed to having handouts for the first week that they then asked me to make handouts for the second week as well. This cycle would repeat itself for five years (recall this lesson again from Strategy No.5: The Five-Year Theory) to the point that I had a difficult time making all of the copies for the students because the stacks of paper were getting too large.

The solution to this problem presented itself in the form of another question; this time it was asked by the software developers. They asked me to consolidate all of the content that I had created into a book, which would then become the official instruction manual for the software. I was beyond excited about this news and immediately got to work. During the time I put the final content together, though, I realized that the book would inevitably become obsolete at some point in the future. Either the software would change, or the way it is used and by whom would change, or perhaps a better 3D program altogether would come around and replace it. I intuitively understood that I had achieved everything that I could by writing the book on the software and that there was no more room for me to grow—I had reached the top. So, I quit. I found a new instructor who eventually was able to take over the class, sold my equipment, and have not touched the program since. This decision gave me room to calibrate my vision for my own future.

Continuously look for opportunities to grow creatively—if you feel stuck, it is time to adjust your path and move in a new direction.

FINDING THE NORTH STAR

Just like individuals, companies too need to evolve in order to stay relevant. You can see this concept hard at work by investigating the stock market. If you pull up a stock from an individual company, and look at its entire history, you will see the change in value of what they are worth. Some have managed to continuously increase their value, while others failed to stay relevant. One tragic example is the entire photography industry, where changes in digital technology and user behavior have eliminated some of the great brands of the past. It turns out that a rich heritage in analog photography products becomes quickly irrelevant in a digital world. The stock prices of those companies show how they were dominating the market for most of the past century, and it looked like they were having a solid performance.

And that solid performance was exactly what made them irrelevant. They were too consumed with doing what they did well. They never took the time to look up and see that the world was quickly turning elsewhere while they kept going in the same direction. They never calibrated their compasses to set a new north, and thus they became irrelevant. It is the reason why investment products, such as stocks, carry the disclaimer: "Past performances are no guarantee for future growth."

I am always amazed to see some companies start to dominate the stock market even though they did not even exist a few years ago. At the same time, I also enjoy seeing how established businesses embrace the concept of adjusting their visions to stay relevant in an ever-changing market. I was fortunate enough to participate in one of these projects that would help to define the future.

The brief came from a major athletic brand that was sponsoring a class I was taking while in graduate school. Our challenge was to design a visionary running shoe that could turn into a new "North Star." A North Star in this context is similar to a concept car in the automotive industry. It is visionary in that it is based on technology and infrastructure that is just slightly beyond the horizon of current capabilities. But at the same time, it should be *feasible*, and thus becomes a vision that helps to give an organization a direction to work toward.

My teammate and I started our design process by reframing the problem (recall this lesson from Strategy No.2: Problem Framing) and looking through the lens of the

Now

THEN

manufacturing process. We established our goal in the form of a visionary question:

What if the running device is a single-material, high-performance structure?

The question has all of the criteria built in to lead us toward a creative solution. First, it no longer describes a shoe. The client wanted a shoe, but in reality they needed a North Star. To me this was the pattern that we decided to break because if we start the project with the intent of designing a shoe, we will likely end up with one. By calling it a running device, we had the freedom to completely rethink what form and shape it could take. This leads to the second element of the question, which is the high-performance aspect. A running shoe needs to primarily work. In other words, if the solution is beautiful but does not provide the performance that the user is looking for, it becomes a useless product. The performance aspect of the concept can be tested with prototypes. The third element in the question points toward the actual vision, which is the use of a single material.

Current shoes use upwards of 20 different materials that are glued, stitched, and otherwise commingled in a way that can never be efficiently separated. In the manufacturing process, shoes are still mainly handmade with few automated steps. The amount of manual labor involved is also the reason why they are mostly manufactured in developing countries where wages are lower. But a shoe that is entirely machine-made could be manufactured anywhere. And with the rise of rapid prototyping capabilities, it will soon be possible to have these shoes be "made to order"—in stores, ordered online, and even printed at home.

However, designing with single materials was very difficult, mainly because a traditional running shoe needed the various materials to provide support, cushioning, and fastening capabilities. That is, unless you design the single material to do all of these things through structure, which was the fourth element of our self-directed design brief. As a result of reframing the problem, our final design process led us toward creating a shoe concept that was knitted together like a sock and supported by a sole that had a structural quality similar to a suspension bridge. It required no manual labor to assemble and was completely customizable to fit the user.

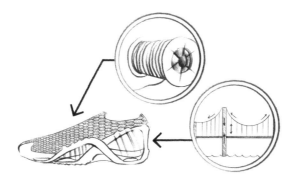

After the final presentation of our design, the sponsor told us that our idea confirmed the validity of a very similar concept that they were working on internally. In a way, our North Star was pointing in the same direction as the one they had already in development, which made them confident that they were on the right track with their own vision. Their design made its public debut about five years later, and since then, the value of the company's stock has more than doubled.

CONCEPT PRUNING

One day, my dog decided to chew up a bush that was in the backyard. I am not exactly sure why he did it, but he seemed very satisfied about his accomplishment. This bush was nothing particularly pretty in the first place, so I trimmed the remaining branches in an effort to clean up. The amazing thing was that a year later that bush has not only recovered, it has literally exploded in size. Prior to that, it had not grown at all. While I was fully aware of the concept of pruning in general, I had never seen the sheer power it can unleash in a plant.

The same applies to working in the creative field, and I have since made this the center of my decision-making process: find the stem, the core, the essence. This can be a vision, a central question, a brand value, or a concept. Then eliminate everything that does not contribute to the idea by getting rid of old branches, distracting elements, and weak twigs. I found that it is helpful here to pretend to be my dog, because he does not feel remorse about chewing up the unneeded twigs. He must have intuitively known that he was helping the bush to grow. This process of pruning can be mentally challenging when applied to stripping a concept clean, because as designers we have a tendency of wanting to add *more* to a project, whereas in this strategy it is about complete removal of anything that does not help it grow.

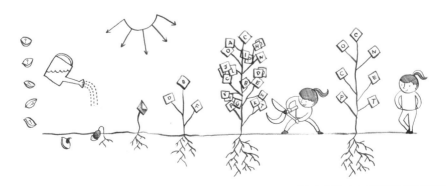

With this strategy it is necessary to develop a deep understanding of where a project (or a design, a brand, a company, etc.) needs to go, and to make the necessary changes based on where it is currently heading.

I call this principle vision calibration and use this both in my professional work and for my own personal development. It helps not only in making some very tough decisions but also in explaining the rationale behind these decisions to your peers that might be directly or indirectly affected by them.

This was the case when a large American car manufacturer approached our Red Thread team to design the lobby for one of their corporate headquarters under construction in Southern California. This was part of a larger, ongoing design strategy that we were developing for the manufacturer. We were to help the architects understand the brand values and how to express them within the space. When we visited the construction site, we noticed that the first thing anyone entering the building would see was the reception desk. Unfortunately, they had finished building something that was reminiscent of a fast-food counter, and to us it communicated the wrong values. Not a great first impression. We knew that while it may seem insignificant to some of the decision-makers what the reception desk looked like, it was important that the vision of the brand was consistently executed across all contact points. In other words, we knew it had to be replaced, and we knew it would cause some kicking and screaming.

To put things in perspective, the existing stainless-steel reception desk was not exactly cheap, even though it looked like it. Replacing it with a new design would delay the construction work, add additional cost for both the design and fabrication phase, and it undoubtedly would upset a few people, or at least the designer who created it. However, that is what concept pruning is about.

Remove everything that does not contribute to strengthening the core of the vision.

We designed and presented a concept that was reminiscent of a bridge that connected both the aesthetic and emotional values of the brand. The design and concept was presented to the leadership and got accepted. The old reception desk was removed and replaced with the new design that aligned with the vision of the brand. While the decision was right at the time, many years later the building was sold as part of corporate restructuring. As it turns out, the buyer was a fast-food company. To them, our reception desk looked too elegant, and it was subsequently replaced once more.

When I tell this story I often get asked if it was worth it going through all that trouble. I respond by explaining a concept that is often used in the German language called "Preis-Leistungs-Verhältnis." It describes a principle of evaluating if something is worth its price. Translated into English it simply means "price–value relationship."

Interestingly though, this principle is not only used to contemplate the price of a banana during the winter season, it is often being applied in everyday decision-making. I use this term a lot because it forces me to take a moment and actually think about if it is worth it to do a certain action. But it is also used to contemplate if it is worth continuing to do things a certain way, or if it is beneficial to shift focus. This is an especially interesting question if you compare the long-term results of a decision (the "value") versus the short-term costs (the "price"). I have found that with very few exceptions, the long-term value always outweighs the short-term costs. In the case of the reception desk, it was not about the cost but rather about making sure that the aesthetic was appropriate to the brand's vision.

THE FIVE-YEAR PLAN

I have found that when it comes to reaching creative goals for artists and designers, it is absolutely vital to plan ahead. The purpose of planning is not necessarily to reach a creative goal but rather to have a direction to go toward one in the first place. And goals can be calibrated along the way to adjust to changing circumstances. But you can only change a goal if you have a plan.

Time is fascinating because we have absolutely no control over it whatsoever. We have a choice to either steer actively in certain directions or to be passive and go with the flow. While these choices may be slightly influenced by external circumstances that are difficult to control, I have seen amazing results from taking charge of my own personal steering wheel. In fact, I have come to believe that people in the creative field must have a five-year plan, at least if they intend to evolve themselves into something greater than they are today. The way I look at it, time does not stand still, and there is no reason for you to be any different.

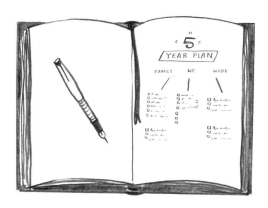

 When it comes to creating these five-year plans, there are many different approaches and priorities to consider. The key is not to make a perfect plan but rather to make one in the first place. You can always make changes at a later point.

I have learned this through observing others in the field of art and design. Some have continuously evolved, and the potency and influence of their creative work has grown tremendously, while others have not tried to evolve themselves, and their creative output remains stagnant. The problem with being constant is that over time the work can become less relevant, because everything else around it keeps evolving. Good designers can anticipate this; they know intuitively how to evolve their skills so that their work stays relevant.

When I ask my students about their five-year plans, I receive a number of answers that we then analyze and discuss to see if they actually make any sense. For example, I had a student once who was about a year away from graduation and answered: "In five years I want to be a character artist working for an animation studio."

The problem with that answer was that the student's portfolio did not have any character designs in it. I said: "No, I don't think you really want to be a character artist in five years. If you wanted to be a character artist, you would be drawing characters right now."

It turns out that the student liked the idea of working for an animation studio, without having any experience of what it is like. After discussing it further, it turned out that the student really enjoyed the storytelling aspect of animation. As most animated stories are brought to life through the characters, the student wrongly assumed that designing characters equals storytelling. We calibrated the five-year plan into smaller action steps that involved getting internships at various studios to gain a better understanding of the workflows, and taking classes that not only focused on storytelling but also building new skills to express these stories (such as directing courses, animation-software courses, etc.). The new plan became: "In five years I want to be able to tell animated stories."

The beauty of this new plan is that it does not take five years to reach that goal—it can be reached tomorrow. All the student needed was a pencil and some paper to create simple storyboards and edit them together into a 30-second spot. As mentioned before, working in the film industry has taught me that it is not the level of technical production but rather the quality of the conceptual expression that matters in creating your own next stepping-stone. (Recall this lesson from Strategy No. 4: Planting Limits.)

I use this example in my class to help students understand the importance of having a plan for the future and to adjust it frequently. To have them think about what is of relevance in their career paths as artists or designers, I ask:

"Where is your own personal north?"

This is not only an important question but also one that should be asked frequently. It is a good habit to make adjustments to where you are heading, but this is only possible if you have a destination in the first place. In other words, you have to know where north is on your compass in order to understand and imagine what will be relevant in your future. This can become an important tool to help in making decisions and finding focus. It can become the difference between feeling that you are drinking life instead of just taking a sip from it.

As a designer, I often got caught up in trying to do too many things at once, and as a result, ended up lacking time to focus on what actually mattered for my future. I have since realized the importance of regularly calibrating my own vision to achieve goals that are far more rewarding for myself. In the field of art and design, this becomes especially important when deciding which new skills to learn that will help you reach your own personal north.

For example, when it comes to software skills, I know that as a student I learned a number of different applications that do not even exist anymore today. Likewise, many traditionally technical skills have since been replaced by software that requires less knowledge about how things work, and unfortunately also promote less thinking in general. Further, many skills have become a global commodity and can be outsourced. Thus, when students ask me which specific skills they need in order to get a job in this changing landscape, I often say:

It is vital to focus most on the skill you need to have for *yourself* and not for a specific job: the ability to constantly envision the future.

And by that I don't mean what the future will be, but much more importantly, what you want it to be.

As an educator, I constantly remind myself that the best way to prepare students is to focus on helping them develop a unique point of view of the world around them and what imprint they want to leave in the world. Change is a constant, and artists and designers are well equipped to cause this change through their work. It serves as a reminder just how important it is to regularly question not how relevant designs are today but rather how relevant they will be in the future.

Your work needs to show where you want to go, not just where you have been.

If you work for a company that does not have a vision, help them create one. If they have a vision that needs recalibration, be the one who creates that shift. Ultimately, though, if you are in a situation where you are no longer being challenged and not learning new things, or if the vision of your company points to a different direction than your own vision, it will be time for you to find new opportunities elsewhere. As much as it can be an uncomfortable thought to make a move in a new direction, I have always found the process to be incredibly rewarding. Knowing what is meaningful to you will help you sort out what is important—and what is not.

And not every plan works out. Even the greatest ambitions combined with a fantastic strategy can hit a roadblock. If life throws you a challenge, the best thing to do is to respond with grace and recalibrate.

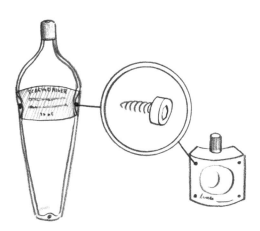

STRATEGY № 8:
SHIFTING PERSPECTIVES

Leave your orbit.

One of the positive side effects of working on many designs throughout my training was that it allowed me to quickly realize and understand my shape of fear. What sounds like a rather daunting expression is a concept that haunts every artist and designer at one point or another. The shape of fear describes a concept where the designs that you create start to look the same— regardless of the subject matter that you are working on. In school we would point out to one another if a sketch done for one project looked similar to a design that was done previously for another class.

My own professional work was not immune to this either. I can often discover similar design attributes across completely different projects. For example, while still in school, I created a packaging design for a set of hotel shower gels. I love packaging design and tried to find a way to go beyond the expected set of bottles. One of the key drivers for me was the freedom to develop our own brand. I created a fictitious hotel called Eclipse and decided to use the lunar phases as inspiration for the actual concept of the packaging. From personal experience I had noticed that I usually use the various shower products in unequal proportions: the body lotion was still half full when the shampoo and conditioner were nearly empty. Combining that with the idea of a full moon versus a half moon I asked myself:

What if the inside cavity of the bottles is shaped to be like the phases of the moon?

This would give me the opportunity to have changing volumes in the different bottles. While this was fun in theory, it provided some interesting challenges from a manufacturing perspective—mainly because my instructor told me that it could not be made easily. As you can imagine, this only added fuel to my fire, and I had to develop a method to bring this to reality. The solution was to approach the bottle design the same way I approached conventional product manufacturing, with two parts held together by screws. Unlike typical products, though, I made the screws an integral part of the design in order to highlight the concept instead of hiding them. The bottles were arranged in a circle, which was a way of paying homage to the full moon, and I also added a diagonal cut to the top surface of the ring that

made the set look like a diagonally cut cylinder. Years later, I discovered that it was actually one of my shapes of fear.

About a decade after the initial eclipse design was conceived, I was commissioned to design a desk accessory as a promotional giveaway as part of the inauguration of a corporate headquarters. The product I designed was a pencil case, and the shape was nearly identical to the shampoo set. But this shape of fear did not stop haunting me there. Years later I recycled the concept of the bottle being held together by screws to design a concept for the packaging of a premium vodka brand. As a matter of fact, if I look closely through many of my designs, I can find little similarities almost everywhere, even though the subject matter is completely different. (Even the reception desk, mentioned in Strategy No. 7: Concept Pruning, was held together by oversized screws.) Naturally, while I believe that each designer's work should have a recognizable common thread and conceptual point of view, I wanted to find ways to make this a conscious decision and not a subconscious one.

TAKE (A DAY) OFF

I have found that instead of trying too hard to constantly change my own values, beliefs, and aesthetics for a project, it is not only much easier but also much more fun to take a day off from being yourself and to create concepts and designs from a different perspective. These perspective shifts have allowed me to approach design problems through the eyes and lenses of others, thus allowing the process to be inspired by a different point of view. Since I am still the actual designer, the project would still look and feel as if it is part of my body of work, but it would have a very different flavor, mainly because I allowed myself to be guided by someone or something else. Of course, there is a very fine line between being guided by a different lens versus merely copying work.

As a design student I would have quite a few assignments that challenged us to produce a master copy of a famous painting, drawing, or design. While I do believe that the first step in learning anything starts with imitation, I could not help but feel that I did not learn anything from that assignment, other than how to copy a master. To create such a copy can perhaps be great if you want to learn how to paint with oil and have never done that before, but to me it still feels like a paint-by-numbers task. Perhaps this is in part due to me wanting to redefine boundaries as opposed to staying within them. I do, however, find great joy in pretending to actually be a different "master" (or designer, artist, musician, athlete, etc.), and then imagine how that person would approach a design problem.

 By temporarily disengaging yourself from the process of problem-solving, new perspectives become possible.

And this works just as well by looking through the lens of someone who is not famous; it can be a roommate, a friend, or relative. The only prerequisite is that the person has to be different from you and that you know him or her somewhat well—or at least be able to imagine his or her perspective.

The design process is littered with potential obstacles, roadblocks, and dead ends. In overcoming these obstacles I like to enlist the use of people who are better than I am: smarter and more talented, have better skills, and more experience, and ultimately are better designers. When I was a student, I would look around my classmates to find the ones whom I could learn from—and often I learned more from them than I did from my teachers; after all, we would be spending a lot of time together. The friendships we formed were based on mutual respect and the joy of working together until late in the evening, and then continuing to discuss our projects over dinner. To this day we stay in regular contact, and when we gather together we still talk about each other's designs and critique each other, except maybe the scope has changed a bit. Instead of, "Hey, I liked your sketch," it is now more like, "Hey, I liked driving the car you designed."

But regardless of where your own creative career will take you, make use of free resources around you: your friends and peers. They are the most valuable resources for your creative process that are available to you indefinitely. I want to emphasize here that it should be a mix of both friends and peers, as friends may sometimes intuitively tell you what you want to hear, as supposed to what you need to hear when giving feedback. I have made it a habit of always understanding that difference and sought reliably direct and honest feedback from peers. It is amazing to see that sometimes people who you do not have much in common with can give you the most objective crits. They are the ones who point out to you what is truly wrong about your concept.

Since being in school, working with my friends, and later even starting a company together, I have learned to cherish a good friendship and the resulting ability to have another point of view on your project. Since we know each other very well, I am able to approach certain design problems through one of their perspectives; and in the process, I alter the projected result. I can also go a step further and ask them for advice on how they would approach a particular project, and if I would follow their directive, it would even further alter the results. Finally, I could go as far as asking them to execute my design based on an idea that I provide, which would still have the largest effect on the overall piece. When working on projects, I was always amazed just how much better both the concept and the design got once it was handed over to the next person. I believe this is because that person saw what was good and strengthened it while eliminating what was not needed (which is a form of concept pruning). The perspective that he or she brought to the project is what made it ultimately better.

CHANGING THE LENS

One of these projects was a small, inexpensive digital camera that our Red Thread team designed for an Internet service provider. The camera was part of the sign-up bonus for customers who chose their service. The product itself was fairly simple in construction, and we presented around 10 concepts (after narrowing them down from about 100) to the client. The big problem was that the client did not like any of them. Or more precisely, he did not know by what criteria to like any of them. We understood that the client did not have the right design vocabulary to express his opinion. My partner noticed this and asked: "Imagine this product as a car, which one would it be?"

The client's eyes lit up because this was something that he could easily answer. He immediately shouted: "An Audi A6!"

I have a feeling that our client was probably a proud owner of an Audi A6 because he answered without hesitation. But what I took away from this moment was an insight on how to approach my own design process and ultimately tackle my own shape of fear. Without changing any of the functionality of the product, my partner had opened up a gridlocked design review, and he did this by merely changing the lens. This new lens (what kind of car would it be) offered a fresh perspective, and it was a simple approach with a huge aesthetic impact. But the perspective shift did not end there because the real design process was just beginning.

 By identifying an analogous product, we were able to reevaluate one of our concepts to reflect the vision of the client.

We studied the properties of the vehicle and analyzed in detail the form language, proportions, and materials. Somehow, though, whatever I was designing still did not feel right—it lacked a certain unity and balance. The solution to this came once again from my partner as he took one of my sketches and some tracing paper and simplified my design by reducing the number of lines used to define the shape. All of a sudden, the product was perfect, and I had learned yet another valuable lesson: a perspective shift (in this case, the perspective of my partner looking at my design) can turn a good design into a great solution without redesigning it.

The design was refined in 3D and later put into production. One of the details that I was particularly happy about was the fact that there were no visible screws on the product. As I mentioned earlier, one of my shapes of fear was the tendency to put screws everywhere as part of the design. Through the use of a car as visual inspiration, we found a way to hide all fasteners underneath the camera body—the same way it is done in the automotive industry.

Vehicles, or car brands in general, are a great source for these analogous comparisons because they have very distinct aesthetics and brand values that together produce very emotional user experiences. The key is, of course, to not have the design literally look like the source but rather to extract and use the *essence* when creating your own design.

 Reference instead of copy.

In addition to using references from the world of industrial design, I also frequently look at architecture, biology, and cultural influences. When I use a perspective shift, it is like taking a day off from being myself. I transplant myself into another person's world. It also allows me to seek solutions through the lens of a client, a customer, a fellow designer, or a friend from a different field. This approach of looking through someone else's eyes to solve a design problem will help your work to be infused with new value and meaning.

HOW TO CHOOSE A NEW LENS

To use the perspective shift, you will need to choose a new lens to approach the design problem. The question is, which perspective is the best one to use? Anyone's perspective can work, as long as it is not your own.

 The choice of lens actually gains creative potency when it starts to diverge drastically from our own universe.

When it comes to designing anything for a specific market segment, I find it useful to take on the extreme perspective of the "super-user." I have seen too many design briefs where the user profile showcases a handsome, mid-thirties, stock-photography person with disposable income and fake interests in life. If that is the person who you are designing for, then your concept, at best, has a chance to be a lukewarm, decaffeinated, nonfat latte. Whenever I see students create one of these, I have them go out and find the real user, the one who defines his or her lifestyle by living it. These are super-users—not supermodels—who are honest, insightful, and are fueled by passion about their environments.

 Shifting perspective is supposed to cross borders, both conceptually and physically, so allow yourself to explore different cultures as the lens that guides your concepts.

You can shift your perspective through different . . .

- **Nationalities:** Depending on which definition you use, there are roughly 200 countries in the world, each with countless subcultures.

- **Belief systems:** Beyond cultures that are defined by nationality, there are also cultures or groups defined by belief systems (such as Zen Buddhism), and I have seen some fantastic concepts by using these abstract lenses.

- **Design philosophies:** Similar to belief systems, there are also individual beliefs in the form of design philosophies that can become great starting points to solve problems. I frequently read through biographies and articles that outline another person's point of view of the design world, and I experiment with their strategies and beliefs.

- **Individuals:** You can also go further and study viewpoints from scientists, authors, and artists. It does not matter if they are famous or just your next-door neighbor, as long as he or she has a strong lens that can guide your process.

- **Pop-culture characters:** Beyond real people, you can also look at icons of popular culture, including TV personalities, movie characters (not the actual actor), cartoon characters, and even children's book characters. Since these characters are fictitious, they provide a certain flexibility of interpretation and can make the design process fun and entertaining.

- **Subjects:** In the abstract category, lenses to take on for projects can include music (lyrics or songs), literature (poems and novels), astrology, chemistry, mythology, history, and nature. History in itself has an abundance of time eras and influential personalities to choose from, as well as art forms and movements that can be revived for modern design interpretations. If you design for sustainability, you can look through the lens of nature and explore concepts of bio-mimicry.

- **Animals:** If you are designing an animal shelter, design it from the perspective of the animal instead of a human. Suspend your own notion of what is "right."

- ***Children:*** Approach a project with a childlike mindset. Ask yourself, if I were a child, how would I solve this? This can give you the power and strength needed to revert back into a state of innocence, where right and wrong have no boundaries but are freely intermingled.

I find this a refreshing mini vacation from being myself as a designer, and it gives my work much-needed strength at times when it needs it most.

A perspective shift is a way to temporarily leave your own cone of vision to infuse your work with foreign elements—and not to feel guilty about doing so.

One of the topics that I enjoy a lot for the perspective shift is to come up with ideas for gifts. The occasion can be a birthday, a wedding, or simply something to bring when you are invited to a friend's place. Whenever possible, I like to spend some extra time and use a perspective shift to get away from the shape of fear, or maybe in this case I should call it the "gift of fear."

Such a situation occurred when my brother was having a milestone birthday, and it was time to develop a unique concept. A friend and I were working together on the idea, and we approached it from a very specific perspective: my brother's.

We did not try to approach the problem with what we liked, but rather imagined what he would value the most. Out of that came a list of ideas that we then filtered through the following criteria:

- **Handmade:** We wanted to make something, and not give an item that my brother could just buy by himself.
- **Priceless:** Though the value of the gift should be priceless, total physical budget was limited.
- **Personal:** It would need to be relevant to him, and for that we would use our knowledge of his perspective.
- **Humorous:** Humor is okay, as milestone birthdays are a way to celebrate both what has been and what will be.

The resulting concept was to give him a popular board game—but with a twist. We redesigned it in a way that every single street name became a street that had relevance to his childhood and growing career, and we rewrote every single card in the game to reflect an important, memorable, or funny moment of his. In essence, the entire game became a celebration of the many steps my brother had taken thus far in his life. The game's rules remained unchanged, and we did play it together, but not without a lot of laughter and tears in between.

All these levels of using the viewpoint of someone else are very effective in evolving your work beyond your own capabilities, aesthetic sensibility, and comfort zone. Being ultimately responsible for your own artwork can be difficult, and this strategy does not delegate that responsibility to someone else. At the same time, a perspective shift can become a wonderful way to overcome obstacles in your design process.

STRATEGY № 9:

REALITY HACKING

Create wonders.

I love reading comic books. Growing up, I often dreamed of becoming a comic-book artist myself. Being raised in Europe gave me access to some of the finest French and Belgian comics available at the time, and I would marvel over the stories, the drawing styles, and high level of perfection. During a trip to America, I discovered the section in the newspaper that features daily comic strips, and one of them immediately stood out for its keen sense of humor: *Calvin and Hobbes.*

It features Calvin, a little six-year-old boy, and his best friend, Hobbes, a tiger. Hobbes is actually the stuffed tiger of Calvin, but he comes alive when they're alone. Of course, I did not notice this because I began reading the comics somewhere in the middle. So, it was quite a surprise to find out, because I, like Calvin, was convinced that Hobbes is real. Perhaps he is. But my real moment of surprise came from one particular strip that caught my imagination.

In it, the phone is ringing, and Calvin happens to walk by and pick it up. Instead of a typical greeting, he spontaneously starts to order an anchovy pizza from the caller. Naturally, the caller is perplexed and does not know exactly how to react. Calvin hangs up, and, as if talking directly to the audience, he says: "I try to make everyone's day a little more surreal!"

I am not even sure if I laughed because my mind was occupied by thinking about something else. That line summarized perfectly what I felt best described the essence of my creative work. It is not about playing a practical joke on someone the way it was shown in the comic strip but rather about the experience that my designs were trying to achieve through their interaction with users. My concepts were trying to make their users stop and pause for a moment and wonder about them. And with a bit of luck, it would trigger in them a question, perhaps as simple as:

What is it? Or How does it work?

Ultimately, though, as a way for my concept to truly come alive, I have always pushed my concepts to the point where hopefully they would cause the viewer to reach a third question, the one that implies action:

What if . . . [enter new question here]?

I think that a design conceptually comes full circle if it can help others have those memorable moments when they look at it and feel curious, want to inquire more, and ultimately have a "What if?"-type question that sends them on their own creative journeys. Granted, that is not necessarily the case with my work; but I think it is a good goal to have, as it keeps pushing me beyond my own conceptual boundaries, to continuously find new projects to work on, because there is no recipe for guaranteed success other than exploration.

I may have tried the surreal approach when I was still a child, when my father took me to a magic show. I came home with a similar line of questions that had me learn, create, and perform magic tricks at retirement homes in front of lovely groups of seniors. In essence, I treat design in a similar fashion as a magic trick: it is easy to do once you learn how to do it, because the underlying principles are grounded in physics and rational thought turned upside down.

The biggest similarity between magic tricks and design, though, is what it does to the user, the audience, or viewer: it causes a reaction, often an emotional one. The piece that was created, performed, or designed comes to life through the interaction of whom it was intended for. Likewise, if I create a design that does not have the potential to connect in this way with others, then it does not work in its current state and needs further development. In planning projects, I always look at what the potential reaction to the outcome would be, and if it makes the viewer/user feel like he or she is experiencing something out of the ordinary.

The design needs to make you stop and think twice, make you feel intrigued, and make you wonder—in a way it is hacking into someone else's reality and altering it for just a moment or a lifetime to come.

The key is to be subtle and not too obvious in curating that experience. Nothing kills a concept more than a literal translation of ideas that only tries to get attention but has little to offer beyond that. An example from the automotive field would be to go out and design a red sports car. I tell my students a story from a good friend of mine who, for his graduation project, wanted to design a sports car. But he wanted to go over the top and hack deeply into other people's realities. What he designed was a "V-12 sports car," suggesting a ridiculously powerful 12-cylinder engine. But his car didn't have an engine. In fact, I am not sure if you could call it a car: it was a sleek, black-and-silver chariot that was being pulled by 12 black stallions. At the final presentation, he had a beautiful, scaled model that was standing on a custom, long and narrow podium with all 12 horses and the vehicle. I can only imagine the reaction that his design must have received (and this happened a long time ago). Until then, the "accepted" reality was that a car concept would need to look and function like the ones that were done in the past. In talking with him about the design, he told me that all he wanted to do was to use his final project as an opportunity to showcase his thinking capabilities and nothing else. He said that all of his previous projects covered the various skills that he had accumulated, so it was time for him to deliver a perfectly executed design that focused on the concept. It worked.

 Reality is defined by what you do, and the goal is to let your audience question if what they see is really happening. It leaves the viewer wondering how it was done and sometimes what the purpose is. But the key is that the result is real, and thus a new standard is created.

In Germany, this principle would often be practiced the last day of school. Traditionally, the graduating students would plan some kind of event that would gently disrupt the normal school day. The idea is to give the teachers some form of a challenge to overcome—after all, they have done an amazing job in challenging their students throughout the course of their education.

I once heard of an amazing tale of a group of students who decided to present the teachers with a simple gift: a car! They held a small fundraiser and were able to purchase an old, yet functioning, VW Beetle and registered it in the name of the school. So far, so good. But then they opted to take the car apart in its entirety, brought the parts into the teachers' lounge over the weekend, and reassembled the car again. The next morning they greeted the entire faculty in front of the school with a small ceremony and handed them the title and the keys. The teachers were left to wonder how the car got into the school—and how to get it out again. It certainly must have been a surreal experience for everyone involved.

PLAY LIKE A CHILD

When it comes to using reality hacking as an approach for projects, it helps me to imagine that I am in kindergarten playing with my LEGO. It is a safe and closed environment, and any idea is a good one because there is no right or wrong, no up and down, and no rules or regulations. In essence, reality as we know it is suspended. This state of mind is incredibly powerful because it can create ideas that are not tainted by all of the extra information that we have accumulated over the course of our mental development. You can notice this very same effect when observing children playing and doing things that would never occur to us. This is because we already have filters in our minds that prevent these thoughts from happening. Pretending to be in a childlike mindset helps to deactivate these filters. It welcomes us to the age of innocence.

Once you rid yourself of preconceived notions, your concepts and ideas can take any shape or form that you like. They can (and should) question reality and not be afraid to break with convention. (Recall strategy No. 3: Pattern Breaking). In fact, the ideas should be able to tip over cows, including sacred ones. Nothing should be off limits, and everything is fair game to play with. Remember, it is kindergarten, and doors are meant to be opened and the contents behind them should be played with. Use a form of planned spontaneity to jump onto an idea and say: "Let's create it!"

Granted, for this strategy, you are not literally in kindergarten, but perhaps your studio, a classroom, or better yet, somewhere outside in the universe. For the exploration of innocence, I have found that sometimes the use of toys actually works fantastically. But it is necessary to define what a toy really is. A toy is something you play with. It could be an action figure, but it also could be an eraser. It is definitely not a computer. We all have seen "creative" agencies that have a lot of traditional toys around, and everyone thinks: "Wow, look at how creative they are with all the toys around them." Toys alone do not produce creativity. But there are tools that help the mind to wander innocently, and some of these tools can be traditional toys. A child can often find hours of entertainment playing with a cardboard box, and not the blinking light sound thingy that was in it. This is because a box is open for imagination, whereas the literal toy is just that: literal.

Playing with objects makes you realize physical and conceptual boundaries and ways to go beyond them.

I love using products, tools, and drawing materials in ways that they are not originally intended to be used. It opens up new possibilities of creation, even if they do not happen right at the same moment but are rather time delayed as the following example illustrates.

CREATE INSPIRING EXPERIENCES

I was having a cup of coffee in-between classes when one of my students came up to me and asked a question about his design direction. I had some ideas and thoughts but had a difficult time explaining them without visuals. In looking for a pen (as previously mentioned, I tend to forget my pen often), I discovered that I still had chalk in my pocket from the previous class. I began to draw some ideas onto the concrete ground, knowing that the chalk would easily be washed away with the next rainfall. While my student received an answer to his design problem, I received yet another question that was going through my head:

What else can I do with chalk on the ground?

During the same time, a large event organizer approached me to provide ideas on a specific conference that they were organizing. One of the challenges they were facing was to create all of the signage that would help the attendees find their way around the conference grounds. More specifically, the conference was hosted on a college campus and spread across multiple buildings. The topic of the conference was sustainability, so the organizers asked me if I could develop ideas that would not harm the environment.

I thought of the chalk drawing and remembered that during one of my visits to the toy store I saw an applicator that allows liquid chalk to be sprayed onto the ground. Commercial grade versions of this are used to spray lines and graphics onto soccer fields and the like. From my early childhood I remembered attempts to use an airbrush to create graffiti-like designs, and I thought: *What if we spray the graphics onto the ground with chalk?*

I prototyped the idea, and after some trial and error, developed a system that would allow an easy and fast application. With templates in hand and multiple toylike applicators, I started creating the signage all over the campus. Of course, when someone is spraying anything on the ground, it can cause a scene. Security came in full force and tried to stop me from "vandalizing" the school. After showing the permission slip and explaining the concept, they smiled and congratulated me on the clever idea.

 What reality hacking aims to do: create a positive reaction in people and hopefully inspire them.

In this case I turned an activity that is usually considered illegal (spraying paint on public surfaces) into a positive experience (allowing the rain to gradually remove the "graffiti"). The ultimate "success" came from the feedback of the security personnel, whose initial reaction was definitely from the perspective of an adult, saying, "You cannot do that!" Once they found out that it was merely chalk, they were all reminded of their own childhoods and smiled.

Reality hacking creates an experience that aims to inspire others to "let go" and get in touch with their childlike mindsets. It also grows a culture in which it is acceptable to take creative risks and to be exposed to the critique of peers. At ArtCenter, the reality-hacking assignments have become a much-anticipated (and sometimes chaotic) event for our entire community.

VISUALIZE THE INVISIBLE

Since early childhood I have been fascinated with what is invisible. It has been a quest to find out what is underneath, behind, and elsewhere. It made me take products apart to study what was inside. Much to the delight of my parents, I eventually learned how to put things back together again afterward. The process has made me appreciate the creativity of the person who engineered it, regardless of if it is as complex as the gears in a machine or as simple as a trap door in a magic trick. This fascination with what is going on behind the scenes has become a great source for ideas of how to visualize things that are usually invisible.

I think there are many occasions where this concept is apparent in the way that I approach the execution of a design. I ask:

How can I visualize this idea in a new way?

When developing the creative strategies, I was thinking about what creativity means to me, and it was based on three simple steps that I believe characterize my process:

Start, create, evaluate.

Dispensing the Unseeable

I needed to visualize this somehow and share it with my community for an objective evaluation. I decided to make some vending machines that would sell these three aspects. I got some old machines, refurbished them, and one night hung them up in the hallways of my school. The next day I would observe the reactions of the students and teachers.

The first one was claiming to sell "creativity," and after putting in a quarter, it would give out a white sheet of paper. To me this was representative of what you need in order to be creative, which is merely the energy or will to do something. The machine next to it claimed to sell "Learn how to draw instantly" and was dispensing pencils. To me this is the only tool you really need to create. The word *instantly* referred to the fact that if you want to become good at anything, all you need to do is to start. Time (approximately five years) and practice will take care of the rest. The third and final machine was surprisingly the crowd favorite and received the most attention. It was dispensing critiques for the price of a penny, which played off the expression "my two cents."

Depending on what creative discipline you were in, you would receive a small piece of paper that would give you a crit specific enough for the respective design field, yet vague enough to fit any project that a person might be working on. For example it would say:

Product design: Use empathy.

Graphic design: Stick to the grid.

Fine art: Make it riskier.

Film: Act it out.

The vending machines are an example of visualizing an invisible concept (in this case the process of creativity) in combination with a transfer of medium (vending machine). There are many great opportunities for visualizing otherwise invisible things, and my favorite ones combine concepts that contextualize time and space and are then translated into a different medium. Some of these take some amazing preplanning, often without knowing what the project might end up being, or even if there is going to be a project at all.

An Education in 3D

I had a moment like that in the very first design class that I had on the very first day that I attended college. Our teacher had us all take out paper and start designing products for the future. Everyone pulled out their color pencils and started drawing. I remember that it was a very nervous atmosphere with electric pencil sharpeners humming away and everyone working as if there were some kind of prize to be won. At the end of the class the teacher critiqued the work, but I was busy looking at what was left of the pencil—it was almost down to a stub. I wondered:

If this is only day one out of my education, I wonder how many of these I am going to go through?

I decided to keep all of them just to see how many I would end up having—even though there was not a particular idea yet that I was going after. After I graduated, I put them all in a box and gave them to my parents as a sign of gratitude for supporting me. My mom used them as an opportunity to create a 3D painting, which now proudly hangs in my studio. She told me that the title of the piece could be: *The Long Way to the Finish Line*, and I use it as a reminder that the finish line comes closer with every step—or pencil—that you take.

To me, the key to visualizing the invisible is to anticipate opportunities before they actually become opportunities for everyone else. I think that the importance of visualizing is often ignored, and its sheer power is completely underestimated.

In that spirit, visualizing things that are not easily seen in the first place provides a wonderful experience to the viewer—almost without any extra effort on behalf of the creator—all you have to do is to be the catalyst that makes it visible. This works equally well with drawing an idea on a napkin or producing a film about it.

Now

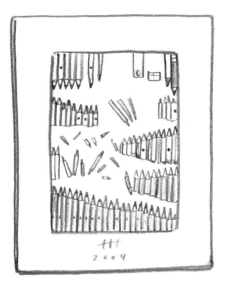

Once you can visualize an idea and share it, it is one step closer to being a reality. After all, seeing is believing—even if it is hard to believe at first.

THEN

<table>
<tr><td>STRATEGY
№ 10:</td><td># CREATIVE REMIXING</td></tr>
</table>

Sample the world.

On one occasion, our Red Thread team was in charge of transforming an ocean-view mansion in Northern California into the setting for an exclusive press launch of a new car by an American luxury-car manufacturer. The main problem was that the entire house had decor that was somewhat opposite to the aesthetic of the car that was to be unveiled. This was unacceptable, as we were closely involved in calibrating the vision of the brand, and we needed to have every single detail of the event reflect the brand values. To make things more difficult, the house was extremely remote without any resources nearby. We knew from experience that if you want something done right, you have to do it yourself.

We loaded up three trucks in Los Angeles and stuffed them with rented modern furniture, flat screens for video projections, and audio equipment. We then drove overnight to the location. For the night of the unveiling, we even brought in some international DJs who would play lounge music on the balcony overlooking the terrace that touched the ocean. In retrospect, the execution of the event probably overshadowed the actual unveiling of the car, and it felt like a magic moment of turning the impossible into reality.

We were told by the client later on that night, over a glass of champagne, that they had contacted other event companies before and asked if they could do it, and they all said it was not possible because there was not enough time nor were there enough resources to pull it off. Considering that we were not even an event company but rather a bunch of designers fresh out of college, I think we did okay. After that night, I began to understand that anything is possible, as long as you set you mind to it.

For the event we did bring the furniture and audio and visual equipment to the location, because we knew exactly what we needed, as we helped in crafting the vision for the brand. But we also clearly knew our limits and outsourced components that were outside of our collective skill sets, such as the catering and the DJs. As the evening unfolded, everything went smoothly (almost as if we knew what we were doing), and we retreated to the balcony to be out of harm's way. There, as I watched the DJs perform, I noticed that the only thing that they had brought with them were their records. This was somewhat of an obvious observation because most DJs at the time played records and did not typically create much of their own music. But I had to wonder:

If all you do is mix together records, then what makes a DJ a DJ?

BE THE DJ

That question was directed toward the skill needed to be, or rather become, a DJ. In observing the performance, I saw two record players, a mixer, and the vinyl records that they had brought. The equipment that was used has not significantly changed since records were first invented, and records were available in various shops. Since the act of being a DJ did not require any unobtainable tools, I figured that there must be a way to learn this skill. I remembered that I did not possess any traditional musical talents whatsoever. However, this was different, perhaps because of the mechanical nature of the tools that were used. So I decided to find the answer to what it takes to become a DJ, and there was only one way to go about it.

I purchased two turntables, a mixer, and some records and got to work. Admittedly, what I created was a train wreck. But I knew that at least part of being a DJ had to do with skills in operating the equipment, and I knew that skills can be learned; it just takes time and practice. And I practiced a *lot*. Every few months I made a promotional mix that I shared with my peers. Eventually I reached a level where I was asked to perform at friends' parties. Actually, I had not yet reached any particular level, I was just being asked because it was a New Year's Eve party where no one wanted to be the DJ because it was much more fun to celebrate with friends than to be working behind a table.

I was thankful to be performing at this kind of event because it helped me understand the symbiosis that occurs with playing in front of an actual audience. Before then, I had only practiced in my studio while facing a wall, so it was actually a refreshing change. And at least at a New Year's Eve party you know there will be *someone* dancing, regardless of the quality of the DJ. I soon found out that for me it was not so much about mixing records together with special effects but rather about curating excitement and energy on the dance floor. I could sense when things were going well and dancers would rush to the dance floor, and likewise when I lost my audience in the transition of two tracks. I knew I needed more practice with more sound and a bigger audience. It was time to upgrade.

In order to have a larger audience, I needed to play at larger venues, and larger venues were not interested in having unknown DJs perform. Thus, I decided that it was necessary to develop a marketing campaign for myself. My design skills once again came into play, as I was able to create an entire identity for myself. I figured that the best way to advertise yourself is to have others do the job for you. I created more sample mixes and also made little stickers with my DJ name on it and gave them out at clubs and parties. I think in retrospect it was the idea of the stickers that went viral as they ended up *everywhere*. Club organizers in Los Angeles started to take notice of me. After all, they saw my identity everywhere, so I had to be "someone." This is how I made it to the big stage of the Palace, a famous club in Hollywood.

At first I landed the very lonely spot of being the opening act, where virtually nobody is present on the dance floor except perhaps for the cleaning crew doing a last-minute sweep. But persistence and continuous improvement helped me to reach otherwise impossible opportunities. When I was done with my performance, I would stay for the remainder of the event to observe and learn from the professionals who would follow me. On more than one occasion, just by being *present*, I got subsequent offers for additional performances.

 Once you are doing something that you love, other people can sense it and want to be part of it.

In other words, I think not a single one of the promotional mixes that I created got me a gig, but rather the actual act of deejaying and being at events did.

Although my DJ alter ego was never a commercial success, I ended up performing on three continents at fascinating locations, such as an old castle in Europe, on top of a warehouse overlooking the skyline of downtown Los Angeles, and in a skyscraper in Taiwan. I had a chance to meet many of my own DJ role models in the process, which was a very humbling experience. Finally, on one lucky occasion, I became the headlining DJ at a major club in the heart of Tokyo, playing to a crowd of more than a thousand dancers.

The club was underground—literally four stories beneath the surface. Within the space there were different levels, and the dance floor connected them all. High in the ceiling was a humongous mirror ball, probably the size of a small car. At some point it was lowered to the center of the club, and all of a sudden, during the highlight of my DJ set, they projected lights against it, turning the entire space into an insanely beautiful environment. I was later told that this rarely ever happens, but I guess the lighting crew that night wanted to join in on the fun.

After that night, I realized that, at least from my perspective, I had found the answer to the question on how to become a DJ: a DJ is someone who creates music out of existing elements, with an audience that guides the process. Becoming a DJ is a skill, just like deciding to become more creative is a skill. All it takes is practice and feedback—success will eventually follow.

If I now listen to the 10 or so promo mixes that I produced during my DJ tenure, only about one and a half are actually good; the others were, in retrospect, just prototypes along the way. I started with playing what everyone else was playing as well. I was making "master copies." Over time you can hear how the work mutates and evolves into a specific point of view. And that point of view was created by mixing existing records into new combinations. By producing *more*, I inevitably created something that was meaningful to my audience and me.

SAMPLES ARE EVERYWHERE

There were some strange moments when I was onstage deejaying in front of a crowd, when everything that could go wrong often did. Preparation only took me so far—the rest was improvised right there on the spot. It can be a humbling experience to improvise, using essentially a small piece of plastic (the record) that creates an amplified sound as loud as a jet engine. Once I had soap bubbles land on the records, making the needles slide off the turntable; I had people spill drinks on the mixer, causing it to short circuit; and at least once I had the stage almost collapse beneath my feet once because there were too many people on it. But aside from the occasional mishap, during the process I learned my most important lesson: sample everything.

I was not particularly skilled as a DJ; I knew no special tricks that one might associate with the act of deejaying. I was actually really conservative, and the only thing I really focused on was to mix one song into another in a perfectly blended and seamless fashion. My goal was for the audience to not even know where one song ended and the next one started. To some degree I tried to make it sound as if I was not doing anything at all. Not knowing any better, to me the skill of being a disc jockey came in the form of mixing tracks together in ways that they would create harmony. Over the course of a set, which would typically last from one to two hours, I would gradually build up momentum and take the audience on an electronic-dance music journey.

In the process, I experimented mixing tracks with different beats, different genres, and different eras together. Some of the records were old recordings of sounds, such as trains and thunderstorms, and others were vintage records that I had brought from Germany. Nothing was off-limits, and the more ridiculous a mix seemed, the more I was eager to see if I could pull it off. I wanted to create an experience that resonated with the audience: a level of familiar mixed with unexpected elements so as to not alienate the people on the dance floor but rather excite them to want more.

I used only vinyl. When I heard a sound or song somewhere that I liked, I would go out and find that record. Once I was stopped at a traffic light and listened to a test mix I just completed when the car next to me pulled up, and I could hear classical music from the other stereo. Even though every aspect of my music and the one I was hearing were opposite, it still created a harmonious connection. I was amazed to hear two unrelated pieces of sound create such an amazing hybrid sound. Back in my studio, I started to incorporate some of the classical music records that I had received from my grandfather into my mixing journeys.

What is most fascinating to me in the process of mixing sounds is that the source material (the tracks) is, for the most part, available to everyone. All you have to do is to go out and find the ones that you want to use. To me it is similar to poetry, whereby the essence of the beauty is, at the end of the day, just the perfect alignment of words—even though they are words that, for the most part, are used by everyone every day. The art form in both music and poetry is the harmony and meaning that are created by the remixing of samples. And this concept equally applies to art and design, and it is the most powerful strategy to produce an unlimited quantity of creative samples.

To me a great concept is almost a paradoxical balance of elements that come from very different directions and thus create a unique bond. And amazingly this concept works fantastically in just about every industry sector around us. Think of fusion cuisine inspired by different cultures, vehicles that transcend categories, and information technology that infuses our daily lifestyles.

In biology, of course, this type of remixing has created genetic diversity that is essential in allowing a species to evolve. Without this type of strengthening, a species is often known to be at risk of becoming vulnerable to extinction. It is one of the reasons why collaborative work generally yields stronger solutions. The same principle applies to the creative field, whereby remixing samples creates a genetic diversity of concepts that makes your ideas consistently stronger. In looking at my own work, I am always striving to find opportunities to add some spice into the mix.

Without the occasional blending of thoughts, concepts become stale.

This was the case when I was developing a concept for a conventional toothbrush design. The original brief asked for the solution to allow for new business opportunities in the field. I began my process by investigating the current state of the toothbrush industry by visiting my local store. For the most part, the toothbrush display at any given store is just a big wall of sameness, with price being the main differentiator. I knew immediately that this project needed a creative remix that would get this industry off its feet and up on the dance floor.

The first step was to identify what I did *not* see, which was relatively easy (recall lesson No.1: Digging Deeper). I noticed that even though toothbrushes have a relatively predictable lifespan, few addressed the topic of sustainability. Approximately every three months is when you should change your toothbrush, which produces a lot of discarded toothbrushes, let alone the resource depletion caused by making new ones. So for the first remix I decided to take the toothbrush and combine it with renewable resources, and the new question that I asked was this one:

What if you could grow your own toothbrushes?

The design was a genetically modified bamboo strain that would grow into the shape of a brush. Bamboo happens to be a relatively fast-growing plant and is generally accepted as a relatively sustainable material to use. The thought was that every three months a new brush would be ready to be harvested and the old one could be composted again—a closed loop system of zero waste. Of course this concept was exactly just that: a concept. It is currently not (yet) possible to grow your own toothbrush.

In an effort to produce a more balanced design, I opted to look at the environment where the toothbrush normally lives: the bathroom sink. I noticed how water drops splashed upward and decided to frame the next question:

What if a drop of water inspired a toothbrush?

As a result, I designed a form that looked like an elongated water drop splashing out of a puddle of liquid. This had the convenient side effect of giving the brush a base in which it was possible to stand it up (much like current electric toothbrushes) and thus prevent the head from lying on the surface.

Next I wanted to see if it was possible to make toothbrushing more portable so that you always have access to it when you need it most:

What if the toothbrush fits inside a wallet?

I remixed the toothbrush with a credit card. The result was a mini engineering task of finding a method to create a functional prototype that was essentially a flat-pack design, which included one serving of toothpaste and some dental floss. This concept was later dubbed the "one-night stand."

While brushing teeth is a necessity of modern life, I could not help but wonder if there was a way to help us understand *why* we should do it. With one of the main culprits being refined foods and especially sugar, I imagined what it would be like to produce a fun concept from a childlike mindset. I have fond memories of being a kid in a candy store and wanted to remix a candy cane with the concept of a children's toothbrush to make the activity more fun.

What if a child were to design a toothbrush?

In the process of investigating causes of cavities, I also found out that, prior to modern dental care, people used honey as a preventative method for tooth decay. As you can imagine, I was rather surprised to learn that honey actually helps to promote a pH-neutral environment, which, in turn, prevents the mouth from being too acidic. In other words, honey creates a balanced physical state (not to mention mental delight). So I asked myself:

What if I create toothpaste that tastes like honey?

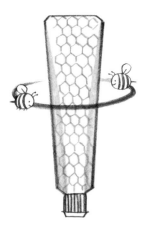

By now I had diverged from the original project brief and ventured into packaging design. Which made me wonder if we really need toothpaste tubes to be packaged in a cardboard box, and I asked myself:

What if the box holds the toothpaste?

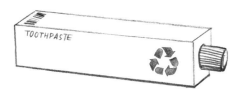

And while I was on that subject, I also wanted to explore the opposite, where the tube becomes a work of art in that it is sculptural and beautiful.

What if toothpaste were a designed art sculpture?

This resulted in a very sleek, silver packaging that was meant to look irresistible and appeal to the business aspect of the design challenge. Along the same lines I asked:

What if the toothbrush was sold in a museum store?

I created a design that had small rubber teeth molded into a clear body to become the cushioned grip area of the brush. Since I am not usually known for producing anything that comes near a museum, I also thought it might be fun to make an incredibly useless concept and designed a toothbrush made out of stained wood and nails:

What if the toothbrush was the opposite of a toothbrush?

This then allowed me to also take on the perspective of a friend of mine who is a tattooed biker, and I finished this series with a brass knuckle piece that was trying to shift my perspective away from my usual results:

What if he were to design the toothbrush?

These 10 concepts were actually an edited version of more than 100 that I produced in the course of a week. I decided to take these to a more refined prototype level to test them out. The problem was that even though there were a lot of fun ideas, none of them would achieve the desired outcome of developing a new business opportunity, other than being rather quirky and fun. I was not yet looking for the right solution—I was aiming at eliminating all of the bad ones first. Luckily I was scheduled for a mini inspirational investment trip (recall this lesson from Strategy No. 6: Refueling on Inspiration) that yielded the necessary fuel to solve this problem.

A close friend of my wife was getting married and invited us to join the wedding that was taking place halfway between the bride and groom's respective home countries: Hawaii. The groom was American and the bride was Japanese, as were all of the bridesmaids. One of them had brought along a Japanese fashion magazine that was unlike any other I had seen before. It was as thick as a small town's phone book and featured the kind of outrageous fashion that one might expect when wandering the streets in Tokyo's Harajuku district. What was surprising was that the magazine had not a single advertisement in it.

Curious, I asked why there was no advertising, and it was explained that the magazine was published quarterly and was sponsored by the various boutiques that were featured in it. As it turns out, this magazine was the bible for 20-year-old females in Japan. It was not only telling them exactly what to wear but also where and how to buy it. Each publication featured three distinct conceptual styles that were followed by pages upon pages of examples on how to achieve the style with various garments and accessories that matched the trend.

In addition to showing the locations of the stores where a shopper could buy the clothing, it also gave the option of purchasing the pieces directly via their *keitai* (Japanese for "mobile phone"). I had followed my typical path of curiosity, followed by inquiry, and was ready for action:

What if I remix the toothbrush business with a fashion magazine?

With this strategy in place, I designed a set of electric toothbrushes that were inspired by the current fashion trends. Each of the toothbrushes came with matching toothpaste to make them extra *kawaii* (Japanese for "cute"). They would be sold as a set in a pouch that was also inspired by the textures and fabrics that the current trend promoted. Since the magazine was a quarterly publication, it would mean that new trends would come out every three months—which coincided perfectly with when the toothbrush would need to be replaced anyway. To purchase, the design users could use their *keitai* to scan the barcode, and the product would be delivered directly to their homes.

The concept was ultimately the result of continuously remixing together ideas and testing the results. It is a process with endless possibilities. The samples used in the remix are from the world around us and available to everyone.

 It is not about trying to find the *right* solution but rather to test as *many* as possible to reach the *best* solution.

The right one becomes clear automatically in the process. Use anything at your disposal for this strategy, including questions, visuals, and abstract sources. I have found that with unusual samples (such as a Japanese fashion magazine), the concepts can light up the room and leave people dancing to the tune of creativity.

LEARN TO CROSS-FADE

The DJ mixer has an intriguing little function called the crossfader. It is essentially a horizontal slider that allows the sound of one record to seamlessly blend into that of another, simply by moving the knob across. Depending on the particular genre of music, some DJs use it all the time, some rarely. (I fell in the latter category.) What is fascinating to me is the utter simplicity of the function yet relative powerful outcome of the result. All you have to do is to put two tracks on, make sure they are synced (that the beat matches), and you can experiment with mixing them together at any ratio that you want. You can have 50/50 or 20/80 percent and immediately hear the result. I use the same principle of sampling in my own work to test my ideas.

This hybridization is a matter of experimenting by gradually adding or subtracting the influence of one of the elements. Often the elements are from very different idea spaces and a forced connection would only create a mutant idea without harmony. I think of this as cooking with exotic spices and flavors; you add them gradually to get a feeling for the complexity that they have to offer. (I learned this one the hard way too.)

 In your journey for a creative lifestyle, apply the same principle of constantly searching and sampling to see what works best for you and your work.

This can include finding and developing a certain style, whether it is a style of shooting photographs (skill) or a style of content that is being photographed (content). Style can include abstract and relative elements such as humor, irony, and surrealism (in a *Calvin and Hobbes* kind of way), but can also be as tangible as certain working styles and collaborations with others. These collaborations can be minimal, such as a conversation over lunch, all the way to full teamwork, where each member has an equal share in the project. Use a professional coach or a passionate spouse. Working styles can be to work in a studio with others or to be working alone; it can mean getting up early or working all night. As far as the purpose of your work, it can be nonprofit or for profit; it can be to help an individual or to help change the world. It can be visible or invisible, made to last or made to disappear.

As a DJ, I used the crossfader in my studio for experimentation, to see what happens when different samples are blended together. On the dance floor, though, I only used it at the very start of my set, in a way to fade from the last record of the previous DJ into the first one of mine. I did this because I wanted to keep the integrity of that last song intact. I did not want to alter the sound in any way, to show respect to the music that was played before mine. Thus, to me, the crossfader has become a symbol of transition between artists and creatives alike. And now we have reached the end of my set and the beginning of yours. As you are reading my last notes, it is time for you to start putting on your first track and start cross-fading into your own creative remix.

Just remember that art and design do not exist by themselves; they are always in need of both input and output, and both need diversity in order to thrive. A great creative person has the ability to consistently channel these two forces and to adapt to their varying natures. Thus, the ability to be creative describes a skill set of strategies that allows you to be ready for any creative challenge that is in your path. And that path, of course, is yours to create.

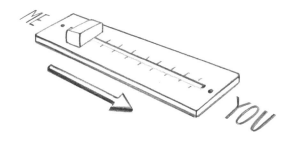

EMERGENCY

10 WAYS TO LIVE MORE CREATIVELY

01. DIGGING DEEPER	*Question everything.*
02. PROBLEM FRAMING	*Change the problem.*
03. PATTERN BREAKING	*Do the opposite.*
04. PLANTING LIMITS	*Use less.*
05. FAIL-FAST PROTOTYPING	*Test, iterate, repeat.*
06. REFUELING ON INSPIRATION	*Feed your mind.*
07. VISION CALIBRATING	*Set a new north.*
08. SHIFTING PERSPECTIVES	*Leave your orbit.*
09. REALITY HACKING	*Create wonders.*
10. CREATIVE REMIXING	*Sample the world.*

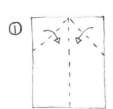
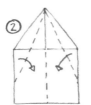
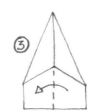

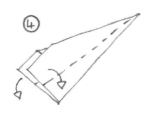

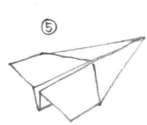

Creative Strategies

Graphic Designer: Prances Torres

Cover Designer: Tomo Ogino

Editor: Teena Apeles

Copy Editor: Sara DeGonia

www.designstudiopress.com

info@designstudiopress.com

10 9 8 7 6 5 4 3 2

Printed in China

First edition, November 2016

Paperback ISBN: 9781624650260

Library of Congress Control Number: 2016954477